D1324867

George Buchanan

A Dialogue on the

LAW OF KINGSHIP

among the Scots

George Buchanan
(1506-1582)

George Buchanan, born near Killearn in the heart of Gaelic Stirlingshire, achieved international renown as a humanist poet, dramatist and historian. His career was illustrious and controversial. Educated in France and Scotland, he was forced to flee Scotland in 1539, taught in Paris and Bordeaux, and counted the young Montaigne among his students. An invitation to teach in Coimbra turned sour after his arrest in 1549 by the Portuguese Inquisition, yet verse-translations of the Psalms, made as part of his penance, became a European best-seller. These together with an impressive body of secular verse and biblical dramas (after the model of Erasmus) sealed his international reputation as 'Prince of Poets'. In Scotland, after 1561, he combined a position in the inner circle of the court of Mary Queen of Scots with a new-found role as key player in the nation's Reformation politics, a balance apparently sustained until Mary's rule was rocked by her husband's murder in the 1567 Kirk o Fields explosion. He immediately accused her of complicity in the crime and (under the regent Moray) helped construct the elaborate case that would eventually lead to her execution. His influence as tutor to her son, the child-king James VI, was both significant and problematic, and ultimate reception of his *History of Scotland* – the major work of his latter years – was marred by royal disfavour when his ideas were proscribed by the State. But it is the theory expressed in the *Dialogue on the Law of Kingship* which is today regarded as his most important and influential contribution to European and American political thought. He died in Edinburgh.

This general reader's edition of the *Dialogue*, has been published to mark the 500th anniversary of his birth.

George Buchanan

A dialogue on the
LAW OF KINGSHIP
among the Scots
De Iure Regni apud Scotos Dialogus

TRANSLATED AND EDITED BY

Martin S. Smith and Roger A. Mason

WITH A NEW INTRODUCTION BY

Roger A. Mason

THE SALTIRE SOCIETY

George Buchanan's Law of Kingship
published 2006 by

The Saltire Society
9 Fountain Close,
22 High Street,
Edinburgh EH1 1TF

© Martin S Smith and Roger A Mason
Introduction © Roger A Mason

All Rights Reserved

No part of this publication may be reproduced, stored in a retrieval
system, or transmitted in any form, or by any means electronic,
mechanical, photocopying, recording or otherwise without the
prior permission in writing of The Saltire Society.

ISBN 0 85411 099 2
ISBN-13 978 0 85411 099 5

Scottish
Arts Council
The publisher is very grateful to the Scottish Arts Council
for financial assistance in the publication of this book

Cover Design by James Hutcheson

The cover image is *Knowledgeable*, an oil painting by Samuel Bak.
The image is used courtesy of Pucker Gallery, Boston.
www.puckergallery.com.

Printed and Bound in Scotland by Bell and Bain Limited

Contents

1	Foreword	i
2	Acknowledgements	v
3	Introduction	1
4	A Note to the Reader	33
5	A Dialogue on the Law of Kingship	35
6	Notes and Commentary	149
7	Bibliography	201
8	Index	207

Foreword
The Rt. Hon. George Reid MSP
Presiding Officer, the Scottish Parliament

The modern Scottish Parliament owes a considerable debt to George Buchanan. The ideas of contractual sovereignty and public engagement, which he expounded in the sixteenth century, are still driving forces at Holyrood today. The monarch is addressed as "Queen of Scots", reigning with the consent of the people. The Crown is placed in the well of the Chamber, symbol of the community of the realm — People, Parliament and Palace working in concert for the common good. Citizens right across the social spectrum participate in the Riding down the Royal Mile which marks the start of a session. And very substantial effort is made to bring them into the legislature, to share in its work.

It is a different constitutional theory from that of Westminster. Indeed, in explaining his *Defence of the Parliament of England*, Milton commented simply: "For Scotland, I refer you to Buchanan". Later, the University of Oxford had the books of the Scots writer publicly burned.

Apart from the magnificent obelisk in his home village of Killearn, his statue in the Hall of Heroes in the Wallace Monument and his gravestone in Edinburgh's Greyfriars kirkyard, there is little public recognition these days, however, of this remarkable poet, academic, political theorist, polemicist and politician. At home, few would recognise him as the college principal who took our tertiary education out of the Middle Ages and into the Renaissance, a humanist Moderator of the General Assembly, a renowned name across Europe, and a tough tutor to the King of both Scotland and England, James VI and I.

As is the way in Scotland, Buchanan is more honoured abroad these days than at home. American, French and Swiss universities still require students to know *De Jure Regni apud Scotos*. In the United States, through the work of his fellow Scot John Witherspoon at Princeton, Buchanan is recognised as a formative influence on Jefferson, Madison and other revolutionary leaders. In Europe, his reputation has been resurrected since Harold Laski commended him to progressives as one of the founders of libertarian democracy.

North of the border, however, Buchanan has probably suffered from his unfair association with the dourer Calvinists gathered round John Knox and the later Covenanting factions. Buchanan never, though, advocated Theocracy or government of all by the Word of God. Instead, as a Christian humanist, he believed like Cicero that the welfare of the citizen is the supreme law and that the source of political authority is the community itself. Living at the time he did — of Knox back from Geneva like a Scottish ayatollah, of a Catholic party gathered round Mary Queen of Scots, of the murders of Rizzio and Darnley — Buchanan required to be a polemicist, a spin doctor of his times, as well as a political theorist.

Whether he ever thrashed James VI at Stirling Castle for advocating a top-down Kirk with the monarch at the apex is unclear. But the quote attributed to him, when the Countess of Mar remonstrated with him, is in a robust tradition unknown to Moderators these days — "Madam, I hae skelped the airse o the Lord's Annointed. Ye may kiss it if ye wish". And in an explanation of the purpose behind his history of the Scots, he said simply that he had written it to rebut "sum Inglis lyies and Scottis vanitie".

Buchanan's view that there was an elective monarchy north of the border from 330 BC is demonstrably thin. But, behind the spin, he had gathered together the essence of a Scottish constitutional tradition and passed it on to those who followed. The theory of contractual sovereignty, where the public good of the community comes first, runs all the way from the Declaration of Arbroath through the National Covenant, the Solemn League, the thinking of

Enlightenment philosophers like Dugald Stewart, the writing of Robert Burns, the Disruption, the early socialist and nationalist agitators, to the Constitutional Convention and its Claim of Right signed by MPs and representatives of civic Scotland in 1988: "We acknowledge the sovereign right of the Scottish people to determine the form of government best suited to their needs".

Almost 500 years after the birth of Buchanan, on the opening day of the new Scottish Parliament, parliamentarians and people burst spontaneously into the singing of *A Man's a Man* — not just the universal hymn of humanity, but a reaffirmation of the sovereignty of the people. I think George Buchanan, himself a member of the old Scots Parliament, would have been fine pleased.

I congratulate the Saltire Society on the production of this book and I commend it to all engaged in the continuation of Scotland's democratic tradition.

George Reid
Edinburgh
September 2006

Acknowledgements

I am extremely grateful to the Saltire Society for the invitation to prepare this edition of George Buchanan's *Dialogue on the Law of Kingship among the Scots* to mark the 500th anniversary of its author's birth in 1506. Thanks are also due to Ashgate Publishing Ltd for permission to reprint here the translation, and a much reduced version of the notes and commentary, that first appeared in *A Dialogue on the Law of Kingship among the Scots; A Critical Edition and Translation of George Buchanan's 'De Iure Regni apud Scotos Dialogus'*, ed. and trans. Martin S. Smith and Roger A. Mason, St Andrews Studies in Reformation History (Aldershot, 2004). Readers who wish to sample Buchanan's original Latin version and to take advantage of a more fully annotated text are referred to this 'parent' edition. They will also find there a more extended account of the arguments of the *Dialogue* and the circumstances of its composition than was possible to include here.

Roger A. Mason
St Andrews
August 2006

Introduction

George Buchanan (1506-1582) was undoubtedly the most distinguished Scottish humanist of the sixteenth century with an unrivalled reputation among his European contemporaries as a Latin poet and playwright of prodigious virtuosity. In an age that revered classical antiquity, and that drew inspiration and example from Greek and Roman culture, Buchanan's mastery of these ancient languages, and ability to adapt and develop classical literary forms, fully earned him his reputation as 'easily the prince of poets of our age' (*poetarum nostri saeculi facile princeps*).[1] But Buchanan was not just a poet, he was also a political theorist, polemicist and historian. In the last two decades of his life, he became embroiled in the sensational events surrounding the overthrow of Mary Queen of Scots, emerging as the leading propagandist of the anti-Marian party as well as the tutor of Mary's son and successor, the infant James VI (and from 1603 James I of England). It was Buchanan who was primarily responsible for creating the image of Mary as a lascivious whore and vicious tyrant – an image first given polemical currency in his infamous *Ane Detectioun of the Duinges of Marie Quene of Scottes* (1571) and then developed in fuller but no less partial terms in the pages of his monumental *Rerum Scoticarum Historia* (1582). In addition to such personal attacks on Mary, however, Buchanan also composed a short but elegant work of political theory, *De Iure Regni apud Scotos Dialogus* (1579), setting out in more abstract terms the lawfulness of popular resistance to tyranny. Drawing heavily on the classical political ideas with which he was so familiar, Buchanan developed doctrines of popular sovereignty, contractual monarchy and ultimately even single-handed tyrannicide which were not only explosively radical in sixteenth-century terms but which fed into a tradition of libertarian thought from which modern notions of democracy, representative government and the rule of law are all derived. It is this key political treatise that is presented here in English translation as *A Dialogue on the Law of Kingship among the Scots*.[2] Before discussing Buchanan's ideas further, however, and examining their subsequent influence, it is worth saying something about the author himself and the context in which he wrote.

*

Buchanan was born near Killearn, Stirlingshire, early in February 1506, the fifth son of a minor landed family that had seen better financial days.[3] An academically gifted child, he was lucky enough to begin his university education at Paris (1520-22) before completing his BA degree at St Andrews in 1525. Thereafter he returned to Paris, where he took his Master's degree in 1528 and where he remained as a student and teacher at the Collège de Sainte-Barbe until 1531. Among his early mentors at both St Andrews and Paris was the renowned Scottish philosopher and theologian John Mair or Major (c.1467-1550), but Buchanan found himself increasingly at odds with what many contemporary intellectuals considered Mair's old-fashioned academic methods and preoccupations. Buchanan was drawn instead to the 'new learning' of the humanists, championed by scholars such as Erasmus of Rotterdam (1466-1535), that sought to recover the languages and literature of antiquity and to replace the traditional scholastic emphasis on logic and theological training for the clergy with the pursuit of classical eloquence and an educational programme aimed at fitting the lay elite for public service. This was an agenda that Buchanan embraced with gusto, immersing himself in classical literature and, through his mastery of Greek as well as Latin, rapidly finding himself at the cutting-edge of contemporary humanist scholarship.

In sixteenth-century Europe, however, the intellectual cutting-edge was a dangerous place to be. Buchanan was eleven years old in 1517 when Martin Luther issued his challenge to Roman Catholic orthodoxy and set in motion the great religious schism – the

Protestant Reformation – that dominates the sixteenth century and whose manifold ramifications were part-and-parcel of the intellectual world that Buchanan inhabited throughout his adult life. In a brief autobiographical fragment, written in 1580, Buchanan recalled 'the Lutheran sectaries who were already spreading their doctrines far and wide' when he was a student at Paris.[4] His subsequent return to Scotland, where he was appointed tutor to one of James V's bastard sons, further exposed him to religious conflict. Apparently encouraged by the king to write a series of increasingly obscene satires against the Franciscan order, later published as the *Franciscanus*, he was forced to flee the country in 1539 to escape the wrath of Cardinal David Beaton. Finding England no more hospitable than Scotland, he eventually settled in south-west France, gaining employment at the Collège de Guyenne in Bordeaux, and it was there that he established his reputation as a playwright, translating two of Euripides' dramas (*Medea* and *Alcestis*) into Latin, while also composing two original Latin tragedies (*Baptistes* and *Jephthes*), both of them based on biblical themes.[5] At the same time, in the intellectual circles in which he moved in the 1540s, Buchanan was no doubt testing, and transgressing, the bounds of Catholic orthodoxy. Certainly, he attracted the attention of the ecclesiastical authorities, for when in 1549 he travelled to Portugal to take up a position as professor of Greek at the University of Coimbra, he found himself imprisoned by the Lisbon Inquisition on charges of heresy.[6]

As it happens, Buchanan got off relatively lightly, and we owe to his two years of monastic confinement his Latin Paraphrases of the Psalms, written as penance for his sins, though ironically destined to be far more popular in Protestant than in Catholic Europe.[7] Nonetheless, being arrested by the Inquisition, charged with a range of heretical opinions, repeatedly interrogated, and finally forced to recant his errors was doubtless a deeply unpleasant as well as sobering experience for Buchanan. It is worth noting here that Buchanan was never a physically robust man – he suffered from bouts of serious illness throughout his life – and equally that as a younger son of an apparently bankrupt landed family he had no independent income. Throughout his career as a wandering humanist scholar he was reliant on his own wits and the patronage of others. In the wake of his experience in Portugal, it would hardly be surprising if a prudent regard for his own safety, and an understandable desire for a comfortable living, led Buchanan to put youthful indiscretions behind him and to enter a more sober and cautious middle age. Certainly, by 1554, he was not just back in France but had found secure and potentially lucrative employment as tutor to Timoléon de Cossé, the son of the Marèchal de Brissac, the commander of the French armies in Northern Italy. As a result Buchanan spent the next few years shuttling between Italy, where de Brissac's military duties generally confined him, and the family's estates in Normandy. At the same time, however, as a client of de Brissac, Buchanan gained access to the French royal court at a time when the marriage of the Dauphin Francis to Mary Queen of Scots was being finalised and when being a Gallicised Scot had considerable cultural cachet. By 1558, in his early fifties, Buchanan's future looked secure, youthful indiscretions a thing of the past, and a comfortable career as a respected court poet in prospect.

That Buchanan now saw his future as lying firmly in France is evident from the fact that in 1557 he had not only received letters of naturalisation from the French king, but had also taken holy orders, entering the Catholic priesthood and being granted an ecclesiastical benefice in Normandy.[8] However, if he anticipated a life of ease as a literary lion at the French court, he was deeply disappointed. Francis and Mary were duly married in April 1558 and, little more than a year later, in July 1559, on the sudden death of Henry II, they unexpectedly found themselves occupying the French throne. But by the end of the following year, Francis was himself dead, leaving the widowed Queen of Scots an unwanted presence at the French court, free to return to her native kingdom in 1561 after an absence of some thirteen years. That Buchanan followed Mary back to Scotland is perhaps hardly surprising: the young queen could continue to provide him with a comfortable living, while he could lend literary distinction to her court. He thus rapidly established himself as a member of Mary's household – famously reading Livy with her after dinner – while also celebrating in formal Latin verse such great state occasions as her marriage in July 1565 to Henry Stewart, Lord Darnley, and playing a key role in scripting the elaborate baptismal celebrations for their son, the future James VI, in December 1566.[9] What is much more surprising is that his return was marked by a conversion to Protestantism – a final rejection of the Catholic faith to which he had so recently committed himself and to which his sovereign and patron continued to adhere.

In 1560, Scotland had of course witnessed its own Protestant Reformation, an armed rebellion that led to the rejection of Catholicism and the establishment of a Reformed Kirk. As a result, although Mary insisted on maintaining a Catholic court and household, she reigned over an at least nominally Protestant kingdom. The tensions inherent in this unstable religious settlement would eventually undermine Mary's personal rule and, for Buchanan, with a foot in each camp, it was a situation that became increasingly uncomfortable – indeed unsustainable – amid the political manoeuvrings that led from the murder of David Riccio in March 1566 to the murder of Lord Darnley in February 1567. Although the circumstances of Buchanan's conversion to Protestantism remain obscure, there is no doubting its sincerity. Had pelf and patronage been uppermost in his mind, it would have made much more sense for him to maintain his allegiance to Catholicism and to continue to benefit from Mary's largesse. Instead, however, from 1563 he was playing an increasingly active role in the new Protestant Kirk, a regular and evidently highly respected member of the General Assembly, engaged in revising *The Book of Discipline* and turning his mind to the reform of the Scottish Universities. To be sure, Buchanan was never a Protestant in the fundamentalist mould of John Knox and, in stark contrast to Knox, never saw Scripture as the sole and binding authority in all things temporal as well as spiritual. Rather

Buchanan's Protestant piety combined with an austerely Stoic morality in a form of 'civic religion' that owed as much to his profound knowledge of the classical – pagan – world as it did to his understanding of the Christian Bible.[10] Nonetheless, Buchanan's piety undoubtedly did run deep, and surely contributed both to his increasing disillusionment with the queen's Catholic court and to his final decision in 1567 to turn on Mary and bite the hand that had so generously fed him.

Yet religion is unlikely to have been the only factor. Buchanan was after all a Lennox man and probably felt some atavistic loyalty to the family of Mary's spurned and murdered husband (if not to the appallingly vainglorious Darnley himself). Perhaps more importantly, however, by luck or good judgement, Buchanan had by 1567 found an alternative patron in Mary's half-brother, James Stewart, Earl of Moray, an illegitimate son of James V, to whom in 1566 he dedicated the first published edition of his *Franciscanus*. Moray was titular head of St Andrews Priory and held within his gift the principalship of St Leonard's College, a post to which Buchanan was appointed later that same year. A well-educated and austere young man, but also a staunch Protestant, Moray was personally as well as ideologically far more after Buchanan's own heart than his fun-loving and Catholic half-sister could ever have been. Moreover, as Mary's regime began to fall apart following her marriage to Bothwell in May 1567, it was Moray who emerged as the most powerful political force in the country. Although cannily absent from Scotland as the last days of Mary's personal rule unfolded, witnessing neither her humiliating surrender at Carberry in June nor her enforced abdication in July, Moray returned in August to be appointed regent on behalf of the infant James VI. As for Buchanan, it was as a client of Moray that he served for the first and only time as moderator of the General Assembly, chairing the crucial meetings of June 1567 which saw the Kirk rallying against the beleaguered queen, and it was as his client – and fervent admirer – that he set out to defend the anti-Marian revolution that had placed his patron in power.

He wasted little time in doing so, for it was in the latter half of 1567, with Mary still imprisoned in Lochleven Castle, that he first wrote his *Dialogue on the Law of Kingship among the Scots*, completing it in time for the meeting of the Scottish Parliament of December 1567 that ratified the queen's deposition. Running only to some 25,000 words in the Latin original, the *Dialogue* is a brief but bravura example of humanist eloquence, but one that shows signs even in its final revised and published form of 1579 of having been written in some haste. Buchanan, it should be remembered, was not writing a measured political treatise, with all the time in the world to do research in a university library; he was responding to an immediate political crisis, furnishing Moray's new and shaky regime with the ammunition needed to justify Mary's deposition, and doing so by bringing to bear in short order – and, one suspects, largely from memory – the fruits of a lifetime's immersion in classical literature. The result is, as we shall see, something of an intellectual ragbag, a welter of ideas – not all of them well worked out – that nonetheless sparks and fizzes to a truly explosive conclusion. Perhaps too explosive: it may well be that Buchanan's populist radicalism was more than Moray had bargained for and more than he was prepared to see circulate in print. Certainly, rapidly changing circumstances – Mary's escape from Lochleven, defeat at Langside, and subsequent flight to England in May 1568 – made it impolitic to air such radical sentiments in the hearing of Elizabeth Tudor. Instead Buchanan was drafted in to lend literary weight to the indictment of Mary's personal and political conduct that Moray was invited to present to the English government later the same year. Buchanan is more than likely to have had a hand in doctoring the infamous 'Casket Letters' that Mary's opponents took as proof positive of her adulterous liaison with Bothwell and complicity in the murder of Darnley. Much more certain is the key role he played in preparing what amounted to the case for the prosecution that eventually saw print in 1571 in successive Latin, English and Scots versions of the *Detectioun of the Duinges of Marie Quene of Scottes* – a farrago of half-truths and lies once memorably characterised as 'copy for the *Sun* in the style of the *Times*'.[11]

Mary's overthrow had left Scotland deeply divided, and the simmering animosities between her supporters (the Queen's Men) and those who upheld the cause of her infant son James VI (the King's Men) erupted into open civil war following Moray's assassination in January 1570. Buchanan was devastated by the loss of his patron, but his mourning was cut short when he was appointed tutor to the four year-old king, entrusted with the education of a monarch who was not just the focus of Scottish Protestant hopes and expectations, but who was seen as the rightful successor to Elizabeth's English throne and a potential leader of an international Protestant movement threatened by Counter-Reformation Catholicism. Buchanan took his duties as the king's mentor with great seriousness, but he also found time in the last decade of his life to work on his *Rerum Scoticarum Historia*, a massive re-writing of Scottish history that set out to justify Mary's deposition with reference to an alleged tradition of elective, constitutional monarchy that stretched back to the mythical foundation of the Scottish kingdom in 330 BC. Finally published in 1582, the year of its author's death, Buchanan dedicated the History to James VI in the hope that it would supply him with 'faithful monitors from history, whose counsel may be useful in your deliberations, and their virtues patterns of imitation in active life'.[12] Three years previously, in 1579, he had finally published his *Dialogue on the Law of Kingship*, similarly dedicated to his royal charge, and with the even sterner injunction that it should act 'not only as a guide, but also as a harsh and sometimes insolent critic, to steer you, at this formative time in your life, through the reefs of flattery' (below, p. 38). In the event, this proved wishful thinking, and James was to react strongly against the political principles that Buchanan sought to instill in him. At this point, however, it is as well to look more closely at the ideas that Buchanan set out in the *Dialogue* and to which the young king was to take such grave exception.

*

Perhaps the most striking characteristic of Buchanan's political thought – the one that both differentiates him from so many of his contemporaries and that has attracted most attention from modern scholars – is the 'secular' nature of the arguments he puts forward.[13] Buchanan is often bracketed with a group of Calvinist writers that includes the English Marian exiles John Ponet and Christopher Goodman, the French Huguenots Theodore Beza and the anonymous authors of the *Vindiciae Contra Tyrannos*, and of course his fellow Scot John Knox, all of whom developed theories of resistance to tyranny, but all of whom did so primarily on the basis of scriptural imperatives and the duty of godly Protestant communities to overthrow their ungodly Catholic oppressors. Buchanan was not immune to religious sectarianism – the *Dialogue* is peppered with anti-papal invective – but his arguments are nonetheless remarkably free of Knoxian appeals to the unchallengeable authority of the Word of God. Indeed, in a crucial section of the *Dialogue*, where he addresses key passages in Scripture that were frequently invoked in support of the view that obedience is owed even to the most tyrannical of rulers, Buchanan embarked on a brief essay in historical deconstruction that is quite unparalleled among the Protestant theorists with whom he is usually associated (below, pp. 109–121). In an oft-cited passage in Romans 13, St Paul had stated in apparently incontrovertible terms that the powers that be are ordained by God and that whoever resists them resists the ordinance of God and will suffer damnation. Protestant theorists, taking as read the universal validity of Paul's words, were obliged to exercise considerable ingenuity in circumventing this injunction, and Buchanan was clearly well aware of the arguments used to counter it. However, rather than following conventional Protestant wisdom, Buchanan chose to subvert it, questioning the continuing applicability of Paul's pronouncement, and insisting instead that 'it is necessary to consider not only his words, but also when he wrote them, to whom, and why' (p. 112). In other words, by contextualising Scripture, Buchanan drained it of contemporary topicality and relevance, effectively undermining the overriding authority attributed to the Bible by his fellow Protestant theorists.

As a result the *Dialogue* is blissfully free of the shrill biblicism that informs Knox's writings. But how then are we to characterise Buchanan's political thought? And what alternative modes of argument did he deploy in developing his case for resistance to tyranny? As already suggested, and perhaps not surprisingly, the *Dialogue* is first and foremost an exercise in humanist eloquence, a Socratic dialogue, modelled on Plato, between Buchanan himself and the young Thomas Maitland.[14] The principal theme of their conversation is the difference between a true king and a tyrant. Indeed, not only is the text structured in terms of a discussion of lawful kingship and unlawful tyranny, but it has at its core an imposing description of the ideal prince. In his private correspondence Buchanan referred to the *Dialogue* simply as *On Kingship* (*De Regno*) and in composing it he clearly drew on a tradition of advice book literature – 'mirrors-for-princes' – that were intended to provide kings and magistrates with appropriate instruction in matters both personal and political. Like Buchanan, writers in this tradition – such as Erasmus in his *Education of a Christian Prince* (1516) – drew heavily on classical sources to anatomise the virtues essential to good kingship, to warn of the dangers of flattery and evil counsel, and, more broadly, to encourage rulers and lesser magistrates alike to pursue an active civic life in the service of the commonweal. Like Buchanan, moreover, they believed passionately in the power of education to release man's capacity for civic virtue and to fashion the type of model citizen delineated in what was probably the most influential classical text of the Renaissance period, Cicero's *De Officiis* (*On Duties*). Buchanan was by profession a humanist teacher and it is no surprise that the *Dialogue* is redolent of a deeply ingrained commitment to a civic humanist agenda aimed at the education, not just of a public-spirited prince, but also of a politically-engaged citizenry imbued with the same unbending regard for the welfare of the community as a whole.

What of course differentiates the *Dialogue* from a conventional instructional handbook in the 'mirror-for-princes' genre is the revolutionary circumstances in which it was written – circumstances that led Buchanan to fuse his Ciceronian ideal of citizenship with a radically populist conception of sovereignty. As a result, he deploys three quite distinct, if often interwoven, modes of argument in the *Dialogue*. Firstly, and most obviously, there is a powerful strain of civic humanism, with strong Stoic overtones, that at once emphasises the overriding need for private self-denial and control – the subjection of man's base appetites to the iron rule of reason – and the public duty to subordinate self-interest to the common good of all. It is in precisely these terms that Buchanan differentiates between a true king and a tyrant – the main concern of the *Dialogue* – but it is in the same terms that he distinguishes between a true citizen and a slavish subject. For Buchanan, to be a citizen was to embrace the *vita activa* and to live a life of selfless political participation for the sake of the public good; and to be a king was to be little more – but nothing less – than a citizen writ large. Secondly, underlying this stern civic morality, is an equally powerful strain of Aristotelian natural-law theory, such as underpinned the radical scholasticism of his own early mentor, John Mair, but which in Buchanan's case is deeply inflected with a Stoic and Ciceronian understanding of the relationship between natural law and reason. Early in the *Dialogue*, Buchanan appears on the verge of rejecting Aristotle's view of social organisation as wholly natural and positing instead a pre-social 'state of nature' and thus of individuals coming together for purely selfish, utilitarian ends – a view that would have anticipated John Locke by a century or so.[15] However, he quickly draws back from this stance (and the Lockean idea of individual natural rights to which it might give rise) and adopts instead an essentially Stoic view of human association as the result of a 'natural force' – 'a light divinely shed upon our minds' – that he equates with wisdom, reason and the law of nature (below, pp. 47–49). Essentially, for Buchanan, as for Cicero, just as wisdom or right reason – reason, that is, in accord with nature – is the essence of moral worth in the individual, so it is the foundation of law and justice in society.

The third mode of argument used in the *Dialogue* – the appeal to an ancient Scottish constitution and the prescriptive right of the Scottish people to hold their rulers to account – is curiously under-developed in a tract ostensibly concerned with the law of kingship 'among the Scots', and will be considered later and more fully in relation to Buchanan's own *History*. Meanwhile, the key points of Buchanan's theory can be summarised as follows. Firstly, he argues that by the law of nature sovereignty must lie ultimately with the people, that the only legitimate form of government is government by consent, and that rulers are elected by the people and must therefore be accountable to them. Secondly, he insists that it is the people rather than the ruler who make the law and that what distinguishes a true king from a tyrant is that, while the former rules according to that law and in the interests of the common good, the latter acts outside the law for his own self-interested ends. Thirdly, it follows from this that kings reign only on condition that they fulfil the true purpose of government as summed up for Buchanan in the Ciceronian maxim that 'the welfare of the people should be the supreme law' (*salus populi suprema lex esto*). There is in effect a contract between the king and the people who have made him king and, if the king violates his side of the bargain, he declares himself a tyrant who may be legitimately resisted, even by force. Indeed, once revealed as a tyrant, ruling as if above or unbound by the law, it is the right not just of the community as a whole but of every individual within it to kill that ruler as a self-declared enemy of the people.

Stripped to these bare essentials, what emerges from the *Dialogue* is a remarkably 'modern' theory of popular sovereignty and contractual monarchy, albeit one that in legitimising single-handed tyrannicide – political assassination – has a potent and potentially anarchic sting in its tail. Certainly, by sixteenth-century standards, Buchanan's views appear astonishingly radical in their populism. The idea of popular sovereignty was not of course new, but among Buchanan's contemporaries it remained largely theoretical insofar as they argued that, though sovereignty might lie ultimately with the people, it was actually exercised on their behalf by a socio-political elite – an inferior magistracy – working through such institutions as Council and Parliament. Buchanan's view of this is not entirely unambiguous – he does at times seem to accept the idea of the people's 'virtual representation' in vaguely defined conciliar bodies; but while he might concede, for example, that the people's legislative authority is delegated to representative magistrates, he clearly did not believe that the people had surrendered sovereignty altogether. On the contrary, he appears to have envisaged them exercising a degree of continuous authority which none of his contemporaries would have contemplated. Such a radically populist reading of the *Dialogue* is borne out by Buchanan's definition of citizenship. Although there are once again ambiguities in his argument, it is notable that in defining a citizen, Buchanan makes no reference to social status, wealth or property. In his view, it would seem that any man, whatever his social standing, has the duty as well as the capacity to participate in the active civic life. If there is a criterion of citizenship, it is simply the powers of reasoning that Buchanan saw as necessary to control man's self-serving appetites in the interests of the common good. While sovereignty lay with the people as whole, therefore, it was to such citizens, acting either collectively or as individuals, that he looked to protect the commonweal of the realm from egregious tyranny.

The resounding endorsement of single-handed tyrannicide with which the *Dialogue* ends, while remarkable enough in itself, is made still more remarkable by the fact that Buchanan makes no provision for any institutional check on individual initiative. One might expect that some collective body, be it a Council or a Parliament, would be required publicly to declare that a ruler is a tyrant and, as such, a legitimate target for a public-spirited assassin. But Buchanan makes no provision for such 'due process'. In his view, a tyrant is both self-declared and self-condemned by his own vicious actions and the people are free either individually or collectively to kill him. Even in the face of Maitland's objection that such a doctrine is a recipe for political anarchy – 'see what an opening for villainy you leave to wicked men, how great a danger you create for the good, how much licence you allow the bad, and what wholesale chaos you set loose on everyone' (p. 143) – Buchanan remains wholly unrepentant. For him, the only – and presumably sufficient – check on the behaviour of the individual is a self-regulatory one: the true citizen, whether acting as a lone assassin or as part of a larger group, must do so rationally for the greater good of the community as a whole. Ultimately, therefore, and perhaps not unexpectedly in a humanist teacher, education emerges as the key, not just to the training of a citizen-king, but to releasing the capacity of every man to participate in the active civic life. Moreover, while wealth and property may facilitate training for public life, they are not absolute prerequisites for participation in the *vita activa*. At least in theory, the common man was for Buchanan as capable as the wealthiest noble of displaying the civic consciousness that defined true citizenship.

In practice, of course, in the pages of his *History* as in his own political life, Buchanan did look to the traditional leaders of Scottish society to uphold the commonweal in the face of tyrannical rule. In the *Dialogue*, however, it is more than mid-way through the text before he turns his attention to the Scottish kingdom with which he is ostensibly concerned and it is only then that he outlines – in notably sketchy form – his conception of an ancient Scottish constitution (below pp. 98–109). He does so in the context of a lengthy discussion of the need to subject kings to the rule of law and Maitland's objection that, while this may apply to an elective monarchy, it has no relevance to a hereditary kingship such as Scotland's where the will of the prince has in effect the force of law. Buchanan responds to this by arguing that early Scottish kings clearly came to the throne by election, but that this altered in the reign of Kenneth III (*recte* Kenneth II) who established the throne hereditarily in his own family, only on condition that he and his successors would recognise their subjection to the law. However, Buchanan's argument at this point, obviously aimed at demonstrating the contractual basis of Scottish kingship, is conducted in highly conjectural terms and the evidence that he invokes in its support is notably thin.[16] Nevertheless, although in the *Dialogue* Buchanan places much less reliance on an ancient Scottish constitution than is often thought, he clearly is working on the assumption that the natural-law principles that underpinned his theories of resistance and tyrannicide had animated Scottish political practice since the alleged foundation of the monarchy in 330 BC. They were, moreover, just as applicable to Mary Queen of Scots as they had been to any of her tyrannically-inclined predecessors. In bringing the *Dialogue* to a close, Buchanan reflects with pride on the two millennia of the Scottish kingdom's existence, attributing the Scots' ability to maintain their much-vaunted freedom less to their military prowess than to the observance of laws which, he insists, are as fair to Scottish kings as they are to the Scottish people. Mary's overthrow, therefore, was not some freakish deviation from either past Scottish practice or the universal laws of nature, but was carried out on the authority of laws framed by the early Scots in strict accordance with nature and reason.

Of course, while an ancient Scottish constitution features only marginally in the *Dialogue*, it inevitably looms large in the *History* and it is worth concluding this analysis of Buchanan's political thought by glancing briefly at his last and longest work. Whatever its precise genesis, and Buchanan's interest in writing a history of his native country probably long predated his return to Scotland in 1561, there is no doubt that in the wake of Mary's overthrow it was effectively re-cast as a piece of partisan propaganda deliberately intended to justify the revolution against her. This was made all the easier to accomplish by Hector Boece's *Scotorum Historia* (1527) which, in its extravagant account of early Scottish history, described how some thirteen of the first forty kings of Scots had been resisted, deposed and sometimes executed for their tyranny. Buchanan was well aware that the credibility of Boece's narrative had been subjected to severe criticism. Nevertheless, though his own account drastically shortens that of his predecessor, he duly rehearses the deeds of the early but mythical kings of Scots, using them to demonstrate not only that the Scottish monarchy was from its foundation an elective one, but also that kings who had ruled tyrannically were restrained, imprisoned and even executed by their subjects. Moreover, fleshing out the argument of the *Dialogue*, Buchanan goes on to describe how, when Kenneth III established the principle of hereditary succession in the tenth century, he did so only by conceding that he and his successors were subject to the law and that the community retained the right to resist and depose a monarch who acted tyrannically. This right, far from falling into desuetude, had subsequently been invoked on at least two occasions: first, in the protracted succession dispute following the death of Alexander III in 1286 that finally resulted in the election of Robert Bruce as king in 1306; and second, in the rebellion against the tyrannical James III that had resulted in the king's death in 1488. The latter event was particularly important to Buchanan, for not only was it a relatively recent precedent, but it was possible to interpret the acts of the 1488 Parliament – printed for the first time in 1566 – as lending the actions of those who had opposed the king complete constitutional legitimacy.[17]

To summarise Buchanan's *History* in such formal constitutional terms, however, is to risk giving a highly misleading impression of its real character. For, as in the *Dialogue*, Buchanan is much less concerned with legal niceties and procedural practice than he is with the moral basis of sound government. The Stoic ethics that figure so prominently in the *Dialogue*'s definition of kingship and tyranny, citizenship and slavery, are equally to the fore in the *History*. In condensing and refining Boece's account of early Scottish history, for example, Buchanan depicts a remarkably austere political world in which virtuous kings live soberly according to the law, while vicious tyrants, enslaved by their passions, are held to account by noblemen selflessly devoted to the commonweal of the realm. Moreover, not only is the political morality of the ruling elite of far more interest to Buchanan than the institutions through which they govern, but it is the moral economy of early Scottish kingship that provides the essential framework for his subsequent narrative. As a result, long before we reach Book XVII and the personal rule of Mary, the civic values of classical Greece and Rome, the Stoic virtues so prized by Cicero, have emerged as the key to the stability of the Scottish polity. Moreover, and crucially for Buchanan's view of Mary, the conflict between reason and the passions on which the political morality of both the *Dialogue* and *History* is founded lends itself to an emphatically gendered interpretation. For in common with his classical sources and educated contemporaries, Buchanan saw reason as an essentially masculine faculty, while the passions and appetites were associated with femininity. It was precisely the belief in women's inability to control their passions – and thus their unfitness for government – that shaped Buchanan's portrait of Mary's tyranny. As his narrative unfolds, Mary is increasingly portrayed as irrational and capricious, intent solely on the satisfaction of her own selfish desires, her tyranny as evident in her moral failings – her vanity, greed, anger and lust – as it is politically in her disregard for the rule of law. Only the sense of civic duty that still persisted in public-spirited nobles such as the Earls of Morton, Glencairn and, pre-eminently, Moray – men of reason and virtue who remained impervious to her feminine wiles – ensured that her tyranny was brought to an end and order was restored to the Scottish commonwealth.

Buchanan's account of Mary's reign may bear little relation to the known facts of history, but it is rhetorically highly effective – and would remain the locus of heated debate for centuries to come. At the same time, however, its thoroughly aristocratic view of Scottish politics marks a distinct shift of emphasis from the radically populist theory of the *Dialogue*. In fact, the *History* is redolent of a form of feudal-baronial conciliarism that effectively re-casts the *Dialogue*'s explosive and socially corrosive theory of citizenship in far more conservative terms. It is perhaps understandable that, in presenting his political views historically, Buchanan should focus almost exclusively on the role played by the traditional noble elite in counselling, restraining, deposing and occasionally killing their kings. Nonetheless, in some respects, the *History's* restricted social vision is strangely paradoxical. For, although the Scottish Reformation is often said to have marked the emergence onto the political stage of a new breed of lesser landowners, Buchanan shows no particular interest in looking beyond the established nobility even to this emerging pool of potential citizens. In the *Dialogue* he invokes a brave new world of participatory popular politics, but in the *History* he falls back on the much more traditional world of baronial conciliarism – albeit a world informed and reshaped by his profound commitment to the austere civic values of the classical republic.

*

In the last years of his long and turbulent life, Buchanan struggled to complete his *History*: the final Book XX simply peters out without any rousing fanfare or triumphant conclusion. Perhaps only the nagging presence of his friend Andrew Melville (1545-1622), fellow Latin poet and university professor as well as leader of the hard-line Presbyterians within the Scottish Kirk, got him even that far. His legacy, however, and his political writings, lived on. In 1583, his Edinburgh publisher, Alexander Arbuthnett, published a new edition of the *History*, bound together with the *Dialogue*, and this combination became standard, the massive historical account of Scotland's elective and limited monarchy – and the lurid tale of Mary's tyranny – complemented by the brief theoretical arguments in support of popular sovereignty, lawful resistance and tyrannicide. But Buchanan's future in print lay not in Scotland, where his writings were banned by the Scottish Parliament in 1584, nor in England, where Elizabeth's government would not countenance them. Rather it lay in Northern Europe where an edition based on Arbuthnett's was first published in Frankfurt as early as 1584, reprinted there in 1594, 1624 and 1638, and subsequently in Amsterdam and Utrecht in 1643, 1668 and 1697.[18] Admittedly, this compares less than favourably with the dozens of editions of his poems and particularly his Psalm Paraphrases that were published in the seventeenth century. Nonetheless, Buchanan's political writings were clearly widely available in the century or so following his death and, though an English translation of the *Dialogue* was not printed until 1680, his ideas were certainly well known in early modern Britain as well as Europe.

Yet how influential were they? There is no doubt at all that Buchanan was universally respected and admired as a Latin poet and that, particularly for Scots, he rapidly assumed iconic status as proof positive that Roman eloquence could flourish beyond the historic bounds of the Roman Empire. Indeed, his status as a cultural icon cut across profound religious and political divisions. It was after all an Episcopalian Jacobite, Thomas Ruddiman (1674-1757), who finally produced a magnificent two-volume edition of Buchanan's complete works in 1715.[19] A distinguished classicist and grammarian in his own right, Ruddiman admired Buchanan's Latinity, but loathed his politics and personality, using a lengthy preface and extensive notes to the texts to attack both. Such a schizophrenic view of Buchanan was by no means untypical, for so long as Mary's deposition remained a sensitive issue and so long as sectarian loyalties continued to shape interpretations of the Reformation, opinions of Buchanan remained deeply divided and passionately held. For generations of Whig-Presbyterians he was a man of principle and integrity, the scourge of tyrants, the fearless advocate of political and religious liberty; but for generations of Mariolaters – Catholics, Episcopalians, Jacobites and Tories – he was a treacherous ingrate, an unscrupulous party hack peddling scurrilous lies on behalf of his villainous master, the Earl of Moray. Ruddiman's edition added fuel to continuing controversies over Buchanan's reputation that rumbled on throughout the eighteenth century and beyond.[20] However, these often bitter debates focused primarily on Buchanan's treatment of Mary in the *History* and the *Detectioun*, and tell us little about the impact of the political ideas set out in the *Dialogue*.

Here, in fact, we are on much trickier ground than is often assumed.

It is easy enough to see Buchanan as a pivotal figure in a tradition of Scottish political thought that goes back to the Declaration of Arbroath of 1320, and forward, through the seventeenth-century Covenanters, to the proponents and defenders of the 'Glorious Revolution' of 1688, the radical Whigs of the eighteenth century and even across the Atlantic to revolutionary America.[21] But this does little more than update a nineteenth-century Whig-Presbyterian mythology in which Buchanan's populist radicalism is played down, his theory of contractual monarchy detached from its classical republican roots, and his advocacy of single-handed tyrannicide ignored. There may be some justification for reading the *History* in terms of a tradition of baronial conciliarism rooted in Scotland's late medieval past, but in the *Dialogue*, as we have seen, Buchanan articulated a very different and distinctive vision of popular politics which was not only unprecedented in its radicalism, but which served to ensure that particularly in the seventeenth century it was a good deal less influential than it might otherwise have been. It is impossible within the scope of a brief introduction to consider this in any detail, but by way of conclusion it is worth sketching in some of the ways in which his political ideas were received and responded to in the early modern period.[22]

There is certainly no doubting the immediate – albeit negative – impact of Buchanan's politics on his most famous pupil, James VI. Crowned king in 1567 when barely a year old, brought up in something less than princely circumstances, James was subjected from an early age to a rigorous educational regime at the hands of an elderly and cantankerous tutor who was not afraid (or so tradition has it) to whip the arse of the Lord's anointed.[23] The results were mixed. James took great pride in having been taught Greek and Latin by one of the greatest classicists of the age, but was also haunted by memories of his mentor's harsh treatment of him in the schoolroom at Stirling Castle. Above all, however, if not surprisingly, he reacted strongly against the political principles that Buchanan tried all too literally to beat into him, but that in the king's eyes threatened the very throne on which he sat. Instead, he developed his own theory of the divine right of kings, countering Buchanan's ideas by arguing that rulers were appointed by God rather than elected by the people, that they were accountable to God and not the people, and that it was they rather than the people who made the law. Moreover, not only were kings bound by the law only insofar as they chose to be, but no matter how tyrannically they might rule, as God's lieutenants on earth, they were owed unstinting obedience by their subjects.[24] These principles were first set out by James in a brief pamphlet entitled *The True Law of Free Monarchies*, published at Edinburgh in 1598, but following his accession to the English throne in 1603, they came to form the bedrock of a royalist ideology closely associated with the fortunes of the Stuart dynasty. Between them Buchanan and James had in effect laid the foundations of the great ideological conflict that runs throughout early modern British history – a clash between absolutist and constitutionalist visions of politics – but one that was articulated in different ways in different parts of the multiple monarchy over which the Stuarts now presided.

It is worth noting that England as well as Scotland witnessed something of a republican 'moment' in the latter half of the sixteenth-century. In both kingdoms, female rule and dynastic uncertainty, combined with a wider European religious conflict and fears of Spanish Catholic imperialism, gave Buchanan's resistance theory and his views on active citizenship unusual resonance. In England, for example, his writings proved highly attractive to bullish Protestants like the Earl of Leicester and Sir Philip Sidney who wanted Elizabeth to pursue a more active role as the champion of international Calvinism and to act decisively against Catholicism by executing Mary Queen of Scots and intervening on behalf of their beleaguered Dutch co-religionists.[25] Likewise, in Scotland, Buchanan's immediate intellectual heirs, men such as Andrew Melville and David Hume of Godscroft (c.1560-c.1630), not only continued to uphold his radical politics, but also engaged creatively and excitedly with the prospect of shaping a civic culture for the new

Britain ushered in by the Union of the Crowns.[26] Yet this republican moment proved momentary indeed: James VI and I emphatically preferred subjects to citizens and, tellingly, both Melville and Hume of Godscroft died in continental exile. To all intents and purposes Buchanan too went into exile, his writings proscribed in Stuart Britain and his name made synonymous with the worst kind of political violence. It was the Scots Catholic lawyer and Marian apologist, William Barclay (c.1546–1608), who coined the term 'monarchomach' – king-killer – to describe those such as Buchanan who by advocating tyrannicide had issued what royalists saw as tantamount to a terrorists' charter.[27] James wholeheartedly agreed and Buchanan's 'monarchomach' doctrines – and the man himself – were repeatedly anathematised by Stuart propagandists.

Clearly, however, neither James nor his son and successor, Charles I, could put the radical genie back in a royalist bottle. Particularly in Scotland, Buchanan's name and reputation continued to be burnished by radical Presbyterians whose adamant opposition to Stuart religious policy would eventually be expressed in the National Covenant of 1638 and subsequently reaffirmed in the Solemn League and Covenant of 1643. As the royalist army officer Sir James Turner (1615–86) later recalled, so universally was Buchanan's name invoked that 'I imagined his ghost was returned to earth to meander a little among the Covenanters'.[28] While Buchanan's totemic significance is undeniable, however, it is easy to exaggerate the Covenanters' indebtedness to his political ideas. Samuel Rutherford (c.1600–61), whose *Lex, Rex* of 1644 is the most comprehensive statement of Covenanter resistance theory, actually made very little use of his illustrious predecessor.[29] Rutherford was not only a professor of divinity but also a man of profoundly emotional piety, inhabiting a very different intellectual world from Buchanan – a world of godly saints rather than virtuous citizens – and looking not to classical Greece and Rome for inspiration and example but to biblical Israel. It is clear, moreover, that both Rutherford and later covenanting theorists such as James Stewart of

Goodtrees (1635-1713) and Alexander Shields (c.1660-1700) were able to draw on sources other than Buchanan in justifying resistance.[30] In particular, they could look to an increasingly sophisticated tradition of Protestant natural-law theory developed by Continental theologians and jurists such as Johannes Althusius (1557-1638), Hugo Grotius (1583-1645) and Samuel Pufendorf (1632-94). These writers were certainly aware of Buchanan, but they were also wary of both his populism and the idea of single-handed tyrannicide, offering far more cautious justifications of resistance that stressed the key role of inferior magistrates in holding rulers to account. In this context, the aristocratic constitutionalism of Buchanan's *History* was superficially more attractive, but precisely because it invoked an ancient *Scottish* constitution its relevance outside Scotland was distinctly limited.

Was this view of Buchanan as on the one hand too radical and the other too Scottish prevalent also in seventeenth-century England? English opposition to Stuart absolutism was articulated mainly through Parliament and relied on a stock of legal and constitutional arguments rooted in the English past. In such a context neither Buchanan's *History* nor his *Dialogue* had much of a role to play. Only among more radical republicans like John Milton (1608-74) and Algernon Sidney (1623-83) did he carry any great weight. Milton, however, was as ambivalent about Buchanan as he was about Scots in general and Scots Presbyterians in particular, and no doubt shared Oliver Cromwell's bewilderment when in 1649 the extreme Covenanters then in power in Scotland refused to acquiesce in the execution of Charles I even when Cromwell held forth at length on the nature of royal authority according to the principles of George Buchanan.[31] Less interested in a citizen-king than in a covenanted one, they went on to crown Charles II at Scone in 1651. As for Sidney, a self-conscious descendant of Buchanan's contemporary admirer, Sir Philip Sidney, he shared Buchanan's profound commitment to classical republican values but in his *Discourses Concerning Government* he combined this with a natural-law theory of resistance that owed more to Grotius than to Buchanan.[32] Sidney wrote the *Discourses* in the midst of the so-called 'Exclusion Crisis' of the early 1680s – the attempt to exclude Charles II's brother James from the succession on the grounds of his Catholicism – and it is no coincidence that it was in 1680 that an English version of Buchanan's *Dialogue* was finally published, translated by the otherwise anonymous Philalethes ('Lover of Truth'), and clearly intended as ammunition for those prepared to go to extreme lengths to prevent a Catholic succession.[33] However, the attempts at exclusion failed and, while Sidney was executed in 1683 (his *Discourses* remaining unpublished until 1698), Buchanan's *Dialogue* was condemned by Oxford University and publicly burned along with the writings of other dangerous incendiaries such as Milton.[34] Two years later, in 1685, when Charles II died without legitimate heirs, his brother duly succeeded him as James VII and II. His reign proved short-lived, however, for in 1688-89, amid fears that a Catholic monarch would re-Catholicise his kingdoms, James was ousted in favour of his daughter Mary and her soundly Protestant husband, William of Orange.

The 'Glorious Revolution' thrust ideas of contractual monarchy and lawful resistance firmly to the forefront of political debate and, in the first flush of revolutionary fervour, Buchanan came into his own at last, reborn as a staunch and vehement Whig, a proven enemy of Stuart absolutism and defender of 'Revolution Principles' *avant la lettre*. A reprint of Philalethes' translation of the *Dialogue* appeared in London in 1689 and this was followed in 1690 by the first ever English version of the full text of the *History*, with a prefatory note 'To the Reader' extolling Buchanan's virtues and the accuracy of his historical narrative.[35] Indeed, Buchanan's reputation and influence in the English-speaking world were probably at their peak in the 1690s and early 1700s when his writings provided the triumphant Whigs with a stock of ready-made arguments on which they could draw in attacking the exiled Stuarts and justifying the revolution of 1688. Yet the political principles embodied in the Revolution Settlement – principles that, following the Union of 1707, came to underwrite the eighteenth-century British state – were revolutionary only in the sense that they served as the basis for overthrowing Stuart absolutism and excluding Catholics from the succession. In other respects the settlement was deeply conservative, based on a restricted franchise and the sovereignty of the Crown-in-Parliament, and extremely wary of the kind of populist and republican politics that Buchanan represented. Moreover, although the Revolution certainly gave him a degree of respectability that he had hitherto lacked, as a political theorist Buchanan was soon eclipsed by John Locke (1632-1704), whose *Two Treatises of Government* first appeared in 1689. Locke set out a theory of natural rights, popular sovereignty and lawful resistance to tyranny that, while certainly Buchananite in both its secular rationalism and populist radicalism, developed out of his critique of the Grotian natural-law tradition and shows little direct indebtedness to Buchanan himself.[36] Although Locke's ideas were no more acceptable to a conservative political establishment than Buchanan's, it was nonetheless his *Two Treatises*, together with Sidney's *Discourses*, that became the canonical texts of the eighteenth-century libertarian tradition.

Yet Buchanan was by no means forgotten. Indeed, while his political theory was to a large extent superseded by the more elaborate formulations of Sidney and Locke, his status as the 'morning star' of British Whiggery became if anything more pronounced as the eighteenth-century wore on and his association with Covenanter fanaticism wore off. Among the so-called 'Real Whigs' or Commonwealthmen, men who remained dissatisfied with what they saw as a conservative and increasingly corrupt Whig establishment, Buchanan's austere civic morality and populist politics continued to attract attention.[37] Particularly in Scotland, where civic humanist concerns fused with patriotic pride in their radical Presbyterian heritage, Buchanan proved a talismanic figure, an early avatar of a distinctively Scottish brand of Whiggery, whom writers as diverse as Andrew Fletcher of Saltoun (1655-1715), Adam Ferguson (1723-1816) and Dugald Stewart (1753-1828) could all acknowledge as one of their own. Stewart, in fact, one of the most influential figures of the late Enlightenment, who as Professor of Moral Philosophy at Edinburgh lectured on politics as well as ethics and metaphysics, saw Buchanan's *Dialogue* as bearing 'a closer resemblance to the political philosophy of the eighteenth century than any composition which had previously appeared'.[38]   If this suggests that Buchanan was now being clearly distinguished from the seventeenth-century religious zealots who had appropriated his name and reputation, it is worth noting that when Philalethes' translation of the *Dialogue* was published at Philadelphia in 1766 by the Scotch-Irish printer, Andrew Steuart, it appeared bound together with John Knox's *First Blast of the Trumpet against the Monstrous Regiment of Women*.[39] Buchanan remained a remarkably protean as well as influential presence in the eighteenth century: still revered as a Latin poet and playwright, he also retained his status as a Presbyterian patriarch, while appealing to those of a more secular cast of mind who admired his rational analysis of the popular basis of contractual monarchy and warmed to his classical republican values.[40]

*

It was precisely because of his protean character that by the end of the eighteenth century, Buchanan had assumed the central position in Scotland's pantheon of libertarian heroes that he would retain throughout the nineteenth century. It was only fitting that in 1788, the centenary of the 'Glorious Revolution', his memory should be celebrated by the astonishing obelisk erected to his name by public subscription at Killearn near his birthplace. A decade later, in 1799, a new translation of the *Dialogue* appeared by an ex-patriot Scot, Robert McFarlan (c.1733-1804), who ran a small school at Walthamstow in Essex. An enthusiastic admirer of James MacPherson's *Ossian*, part of which he translated into Latin, he was equally an enthusiast for Buchanan whom he described as nothing less than 'the father of politics in modern Europe'.[41] The claim, though echoing the remarks of Dugald Stewart, is doubtless an exaggerated one. Nevertheless, Buchanan's significance in the history of western political thought in general and the British libertarian tradition in particular should not be underestimated. Unfortunately, in the course of the last century or so, interest in Buchanan has declined along with interest in the classical languages and cultures he did so much to champion. While Peter Hume Brown wrote a spirited and sympathetic biography of him in 1890, and the 1906 quatercentenary of his birth witnessed a series of grand celebratory events, Buchanan has subsequently dropped out of public consciousness more or less altogether.[42] Among modern scholars, however, he is routinely recognised as one of the most innovative as well as the most radical political theorists of the sixteenth century, propounding theories of popular sovereignty and contractual monarchy that were in many respects well ahead of their time but that have proved fundamental in shaping modern understanding of democracy and representative government. His *Dialogue on the Law of Kingship among the Scots* deserves to be taken seriously both as a remarkable example of sixteenth-century civic humanism and as a key text in the history of western libertarian thinking.

Notes on the Introduction

[1] The accolade originated with Buchanan's publishers, the Estienne brothers, but it was a description that stuck and continues to be widely used of him; see, for example, P. J. Ford and W. S. Watt, *George Buchanan, 'Prince of Poets', with an Edition of the 'Miscellaneorum Liber'* (Aberdeen, 1982).

[2] The translation first appeared together with the Latin original in *A Dialogue on the Law of Kingship among the Scots; A Critical Edition and Translation of George Buchanan's 'De Iure Regni apud Scotos Dialogus'*, ed. and trans. R. A. Mason and M. S. Smith (Aldershot, 2004).

[3] The standard biography is I. D. McFarlane's encyclopaedic *Buchanan* (London, 1981).

[4] For an English translation of Buchanan's *Vita*, see J. M. Aitken (ed.), *The Trial of George Buchanan Before the Lisbon Inquisition* (Edinburgh, 1939), pp. xiv-xxvii.

[5] For a modern edition of all four plays, see P. Sharratt and P. G. Walsh (eds.), *George Buchanan Tragedies* (Edinburgh, 1983).

[6] For full details, see Aitken, *Trial of George Buchanan*.

[7] For full details of editions of the Psalms as well as of all Buchanan's other published writings, see J. Durkan's invaluable *Bibliography of George Buchanan* (Glasgow, 1994).

[8] That Buchanan entered the Catholic priesthood was not known to his earlier biographers, but see E. Bonner, 'French Naturalisation of the Scots in the Fifteenth and Sixteenth Centuries', *Historical Journal*, 40 (1997), pp. 1085-1115.

[9] See P. Davidson, D. Montserrat and J. Stevenson, 'Three Entertainments for the Wedding of Mary Queen of Scots Written

by George Buchanan', *Scotlands*, 2 (1995), pp. 1-10; and M. Lynch, 'Queen Mary's Triumph: The Baptismal Celebrations at Stirling in December 1566', *Scottish Historical Review*, 69 (1990), pp. 1-21.

[10] On Buchanan's *pietas*, see in particular the introduction to George Buchanan, *The Political Poetry*, ed. and trans. A. H. Williamson and P. G. McGinnis (Edinburgh, 1995), especially pp. 28-9.

[11] J. Wormald, *Mary Queen of Scots: A Study in Failure* (London, 1988), p. 14. For the text of the *Detectioun* and a close analysis of its relationship with the relevant books of the *Historia Rerum Scoticarum*, see W. A. Gatherer (ed.), *The Tyrannous Reign of Mary Queen of Scots: George Buchanan's Account* (Edinburgh, 1958).

[12] George Buchanan, *The History of Scotland*, trans. J. Aikman (4 vols., Glasgow, 1827), I, pp. ciii-civ.

[13] For general background, see Q. Skinner, *The Foundations of Modern Political Thought* (2 vols., Cambridge, 1978), esp. II, chs. 7-9, and J. H. Burns (ed.), *The Cambridge History of Political Thought, 1450–1700* (Cambridge, 1991), esp. chs. 6-8. More specific studies of Scottish political thought include: A. H. Williamson, *Scottish National Consciousness in the Age of James VI* (Edinburgh, 1979); J. H. Burns, *The True Law of Kingship: Concepts of Monarchy in Early Modern Scotland* (Oxford, 1996); and R. A. Mason, *Kingship and the Commonweal: Political Thought in Renaissance and Reformation Scotland* (East Linton, 1998).

[14] Thomas Maitland, brother of the much better known William Maitland of Lethington, was a student in Paris in the 1560s and probably did return to Scotland in 1567. The Maitland family supported the revolution against Mary but subsequently defected to the Queen's Party and Thomas later denied having taken part in any such conversation with Buchanan. He died en route to Rome in 1572, while William held Edinburgh Castle for the Queen until its capture in 1573 and his own death, possibly by suicide. See W. S. McKechnie, 'Thomas Maitland', *Scottish Historical Review*, 4 (1906–7), pp. 274-93.

[15] For an important discussion of this, see J. H. M. Salmon, 'An Alternative Theory of Popular Resistance: Buchanan, Rossaeus and Locke', in J. H. M. Salmon, *Renaissance and Revolt: Essays in the Intellectual and Social History of Early Modern France* (Cambridge, 1987), pp. 136-54.

[16] It has been argued that, by the time he published the *Dialogue* in 1579, Buchanan's earlier enthusiasm for an ancient Scottish constitution had been deflated by attacks on the credibility of the ancient line of kings: see H. R. Trevor-Roper, 'George Buchanan and the Ancient Scottish Constitution', *English Historical Review*, Supplement 3 (1966). However, there is little evidence that Buchanan revised the text substantially between its original composition in 1567 and its publication twelve years later. The lack of reliance on arguments from the remote Scottish past is more likely the result of Buchanan self-consciously addressing a European audience in terms that would resonate with fellow humanists unfamiliar with the fate of obscure Scottish monarchs such as Evenus, Ferquhard and Culenus.

[17] See *The Actis and Constitutionis of the Realme of Scotland* (Edinburgh, 1566). For more detailed consideration of Buchanan's historical arguments, see the notes to the text.

[18] For full details of these editions, see Durkan, *Bibliography*, pp. 209ff.

[19] *Georgii Buchanani, Scoti ... Opera Omnia*, ed. Thomas Ruddiman (2 vols., Edinburgh, 1715). For background, see D. Duncan, *Thomas Ruddiman: A Study in Scottish Scholarship of the Early Eighteenth Century* (London, 1965), pp. 62-71.

[20] On these debates, see in particular C. Kidd, *Subverting Scotland's Past: Scottish Whig Historians and the Creation of an Anglo-British Identity, 1689-c.1830* (Cambridge, 1993).

[21] For a recent example, see E. J. Cowan, *'For Freedom Alone': The Declaration of Arbroath, 1320* (East Linton, 2003).

[22] For a full and illuminating discussion, see C. Erskine, 'The Reputation of George Buchanan (1506-1582) in the British Atlantic World before 1832' (Unpublished PhD Thesis, University of Glasgow, 2005).

[23] For this and what follows, see Mason, *Kingship and the Commonweal*, chs. 7-8.

[24] For James's writings on kingship, see J. Craigie (ed.), *Minor Prose Works of King James VI and I* (Scottish Text Society, 1982).

[25] See J. E. Phillips, 'George Buchanan and the Sidney Circle', *Huntington Library Quarterly*, 12 (1948-49), pp. 23-55.

[26] See the introduction to A. H. Williamson and P. J. McGinnis (eds.), *The British Union: A Critical Edition and Translation of David Hume of Godscroft's 'De Unione Insulae Britannicae'* (Aldershot, 2002).

[27] William Barclay, *De Regno et Regali Potestate Adversus Buchananum, Brutum, Boucherium & Reliquos Monarchomachos* (Paris, 1600).

[28] Quoted in Gatherer (ed.), *Tyrannous Reign*, p. 5.

[29] Samuel Rutherford, *Lex, Rex. Or, The Law and the Prince; A Dispute for the Just Prerogative of King and People* (London, 1644). For an excellent analysis of Rutherford's thought, see J. Coffey, *Politics, Religion and the British Revolutions: The Mind of Samuel Rutherford* (Cambridge, 1997).

[30] Sir James Stewart, *Ius Populi Vindicatum. Or, The People's Right to Defend Themselves and Their Covenanted Religion* (Edinburgh, 1669); Alexander Shields, *A Hind Let Loose. Or, An Historical Representation of the Testimonies of the Church of Scotland for the Interest of Christ* (Edinburgh, 1687).

[31] W. C. Abbott (ed.), *The Writings and Speeches of Oliver Cromwell* (Cambridge, Mass., 1937-47), I, p. 746.

[32] See John Milton, *Political Writings*, ed. M. Dzelzainis (Cambridge, 1991).

[33] *De Iure Regni apud Scotos.Or, A Dialogue Concerning the Due Priviledge of Government in the Kingdom of Scotland... translated out of the Original Latine into English by PHILALETHES* (London, 1680).

[34] At the same time, in Scotland, Sir George Mackenzie of Rosehaugh (c.1638-91) responded to the appearance of the English *Dialogue* by re-stating in his *Ius Regium: Or the Just and Solid Foundations of Monarchy in General; and more especially of the Monarchy of Scotland* of 1684 the arguments for the divine, absolute and irresistible nature of royal authority.

[35] Missing no opportunity to smear the Stuarts, a new edition of the *Detectioun* was also published in 1689. For details of these editions, see Durkan, *Bibliography*, pp. 207, 216, 234.

[36] John Locke, *Two Treatises of Government*, ed. P. Laslett (2nd edn, Cambridge, 1967).

[37] C. Robbins, *The Eighteenth Century Commonwealthman* (New York, 1968).

[38] Quoted in *ibid.*, p. 179.

[39] *De Iure Regni Apud Scotos. Or, A Dialogue, Concerning the Due Privilege of Government, in the Kingdom of Scotland* (Philadelphia, 1766).

[40] For a useful recent survey of Buchanan's importance in these traditions, see L. McIlvanney, *Burns the Radical: Poetry and Politics in Late Eighteenth-Century Scotland* (East Linton, 2002).

[41] George Buchanan's *Dialogue Concerning the Rights of the Crown of Scotland translated into English; with two dissertations prefixed; one archeological... and the other historical... by Robert MacFarlan, A.M.* (London and Edinburgh, 1799), p. 64.

[42] P. H. Brown, *George Buchanan: Humanist and Reformer* (Edinburgh, 1890); *George Buchanan: Glasgow Quatercentenary Studies, 1906* (Glasgow, 1907).

A Note to the Reader

The first edition of the *De Iure Regni apud Scotos Dialogus* appeared at Edinburgh in 1579 and was subsequently reissued the same year, and again in 1580. These reprints are essentially identical to the first edition which forms the basis of the current translation. While manuscript copies of the text certainly circulated prior to its publication in 1579, only one is known to have survived (British Library Add MS 48043, Yelverton MS 48, fos. 123-152) in a collection of political tracts assembled by the Englishman Robert Beale in 1577 or 1578. The manuscript lacks the dedication to James VI and the lines from Seneca's *Thyestes* at the end of the text found in all printed editions. However, it does contain one passage of some twenty lines as well as a number of other phrases and sentences which do not appear in the printed edition and which would seem to confirm that the clerk was copying a version of the text which was subsequently revised for publication. This is borne out by the many minor variations between the manuscript and printed versions that might be construed as stylistic changes rather than scribal errors. While the latter predominate, there are instances – changes in word order, the substitution of one word for another, and the deletion of the passages mentioned above – which suggest a deliberate if fairly light and perhaps hurried process of revision for publication. These deleted passages are reinstated here, italicised in square brackets to distinguish them from what appeared in print in 1579.

The aim of the translation is to render Buchanan's original Latin into English as clearly and concisely as possible. Rather than attempting to capture the spirit or rhythms of Buchanan's Latin, we have preferred to err on the side of caution and provide as exact and literal a version as possible. We have also tried to avoid introducing modern and potentially anachronistic usages. Translation, however, is hardly an exact science and there are inevitably words and phrases that remain problematic. The title itself is a case in point: while earlier translators have exercised considerable ingenuity in rendering *De Iure Regni*, we have preferred the more literal *The Law of Kingship*. Latin words such as *civis* and *respublica* as well as *ius* had more or less specialised meanings in the sixteenth-century humanist vocabulary and have been translated here in various ways depending on the context in which they occur. Where particular difficulties occur in translating the Latin, this is explained in the notes.

The original Latin version of the text was printed as a continuous dialogue. To ease the reader's path through Buchanan's argument, however, breaks have been introduced that are intended to bring out the underlying structure of the conversation. As noted in the introduction, the main focus of the discussion is the difference between kingship and tyranny, and approximately half of the text is devoted to each them. In the first half, following some brief scene-setting preliminaries (pp. 40–46), Buchanan proceeds to an analysis of the origins of social organisation and political authority (pp. 46–65); a discussion of the need to subject rulers to the authority of the law (pp. 65–82); and a description of an ideal king (pp. 83–90). The second half is more complex but is essentially made up of a contrast between a king ruling according to law and a tyrant who ignores it (pp. 90–98); a discussion of how tyrants may be restrained in a kingdom such as Scotland where the monarchy is hereditary rather than elective (pp. 98–109); a lengthy digression on scriptural arguments in favour of obedience even to tyrants (pp. 109–121); and finally the development of the natural-law principles that legitimise resistance and tyrannicide and on which the Scottish constitution is said to be founded (pp. 121–147). Further guidance will be found in the Notes and Commentary.

GEORGE BUCHANAN

A Dialogue on the
Law of Kingship
among the Scots

George Buchanan to James VI, King of Scots, Greetings

Some years ago, when our country's affairs were in a very unsettled state, I wrote a dialogue concerning the right of the kings of Scots in which I tried to explain from their very cradle (if I may put it that way) the mutual rights or powers of kings and their subjects. At the time the book seemed to have been of some use in silencing certain people who railed against the existing situation with unseemly cries rather than weighing what was right in the scale of reason. But as our affairs became a little more tranquil, I too put aside my arms and willingly laid them upon the altar of public concord. Recently, however, I happened to find that discussion among my papers, and seeming to find in it many things which were necessary to someone of your age (and especially to someone with your role in public life), I decided to publish it both to witness to my zeal for you and to advise you of your duty towards your subjects. Many things make me confident that this effort of mine will not be wasted. Your age in particular, not yet corrupted by vicious opinion; a character far above your years, eager of its own accord to strive for distinction of every kind; a willingness to submit not only to your teachers but to all those who give you good advice; and such judgement and skill in assessing matters that no man's authority carries much weight with you in anything unless it is supported by sound reasoning. I also see that by a certain natural instinct you so abhor flattery, the nurse of tyranny and the most grievous plague of lawful kingship, that you despise the solecisms and barbarisms of courtiers no less than they are relished and affected by those who, seeing themselves as arbiters of all good taste, randomly sprinkle their conversation, as if it were seasoning, with 'majesties', 'lordships', 'excellencies', and other terms which are even more repugnant. Although your natural goodness and the teaching of your instructors protect you for the present from this error, nevertheless I am bound to be somewhat anxious lest evil company, the fawning foster-mother of the vices, should twist your still tender mind in the worse direction, especially since I know how readily our other senses yield to temptation. I have sent you this book, then, not only as a guide, but also as a harsh and sometimes insolent critic, to steer you, at this formative time in your life, through the reefs of flattery. It may not only admonish you, but also keep you to the path which you have once embarked upon, and if you should stray from it, rebuke you and drag you back again. If you obey it, you will gain for yourself and your people tranquillity in the present and, in the future, everlasting glory.

Farewell.

From Stirling. In the year of human salvation 1579, the 10th day of January.

A Dialogue on the Law of Kingship among the Scots, written by George Buchanan, a Scot

THE CHARACTERS
George Buchanan and Thomas Maitland

Soon after Thomas Maitland's return from France I questioned him closely about the situation there.[1] In my regard for him I began by encouraging him to continue on his chosen path to glory and to be full of confidence in the success of his studies: 'For I myself am a man of modest ability and almost no resources and I was born in an uncultured age, yet I seem to have achieved something in my struggle against unfavourable circumstances. Surely, then, those born in a more fortunate age and enjoying youth, wealth and ability in abundance, should not be deterred from a noble enterprise by the labour involved, and with so many advantages on their side they have no reason to despair. They should strive to the utmost to enhance the world of literature and to win for themselves and their fellow-countrymen a place in the memory of posterity. If they were to make even the slightest effort, they would put an end to the notion that in the colder parts of the world men are as far removed from learning, culture and every form of intellectual pursuit as they are from the sun. Nature may have bestowed nimbler wits and keener intellects on the Africans, Egyptians and many other peoples, but it has not so utterly condemned any race as to deprive it of all access to virtue and renown.'[2]

Thereupon, with his usual modesty, he was unassuming in speaking of himself, and more affectionate than truthful when he spoke of me. Eventually, the course of our conversation led him to ask me about the troubled state of our country, and I answered him as fully as seemed appropriate to the occasion. In turn, I began to ask him just what was the view of our affairs held by the French or other peoples he had met in France. For I was in no doubt that the very novelty of what had happened would, as usual, have provided everyone with scope and opportunity for gossip. 'Why do you ask me that?', he said. 'You know the course of events and are well aware what most men are saying and almost all of them are thinking, so you can easily guess from what you already know what the general view is, or at least what it ought to be.'

BUCHANAN: But the further away foreign countries lie, and hence the fewer reasons they have for anger, hatred, love and other emotions which can deflect the mind from the truth, the sounder generally is their judgement and the freer they are to express their feelings. That same freedom of speech and discussion brings many obscurities to light, explains difficulties and clears up doubts; it can silence the tongues of the wicked and give instruction to the weak.

MAITLAND: Would you like me to be candid with you?

B. Of course.

M. Although after so long a time I was extremely anxious to see my country, my parents, my kinsmen and my friends, nothing fired this longing as much as the outcry of the ignorant mob. I had thought my character hardened by habit and by the teaching of men of the greatest learning, but when it came to the present situation somehow I could not conceal how sensitive my feelings were. With one voice everyone condemned the foul deed committed here not so long before. But it was unclear who was responsible for it, and the common people, carried away by impulse rather than ruled by reason, blamed all of us for what a few had done. The general odium arising from the crime of individuals so recoiled against our whole nation that even those most above suspicion were tainted with the infamy of someone else's evil act.[3] To allow what I might call this storm of misrepresentation to subside, therefore, I gladly took refuge in this harbour. In doing so, however, I fear I may have struck a reef.

B. Why is that?

M. Because, with everyone's feelings already kindled against us, the enormity of the recent crime seems to me to have so inflamed them that now there is no room left to mount a defence.[4] For how can I put up any resistance when I am attacked not just by the ignorant but by those who think they know better? They will cry out that, not content to murder an innocent youth with unheard of cruelty, we would commit against women (a sex spared by the enemy even when cities are captured) an act of unparalleled barbarity: 'What villainy will any rank or majesty deter them from if they vent their rage against their kings in this way? What place does compassion have among those who are restrained neither by regard for the weaker sex nor by the innocence of youth? Right, custom, laws, respect for authority, reverence for a lawful magistrate – whom, after this, will any of these curb through shame or coerce by fear, when the power of the supreme authority is subjected to the mockery of the meanest of men? Or when the distinction between right and wrong, honour and dishonour, is once removed, and things degenerate almost by common consent into savage barbarity?' I know that when I return to France I shall hear these and harsher charges, all men's ears being closed for the moment and no defence or explanation being heard.

B. But I shall easily rid you of this fear and clear our nation of this spurious charge. For if they detest the cruelty of the first crime so much, how can they reasonably criticise the severity used in avenging it? Or if they are angry at the queen being deposed, they must necessarily approve of the earlier deed.[5] Choose, then, which of the two you want to be regarded as barbarous. For neither your critics nor you (if you want to be consistent) can praise or censure both.

M. Certainly I abhor and detest the murder of the king and am glad that the odium of it has been lifted from the public conscience and ascribed to the depravity of a few. Yet this later action I can neither condemn nor praise without qualification. I think it a splendid and memorable achievement that by their wisdom and diligence they have brought to light the most heinous crime in the whole history of man and are pursuing the miscreants with armed force. But I am unsure how all the nations of Europe, especially those living under royal authority, will react to their deposition of the supreme magistrate and their contempt for the name of king, which every people has at all times held to be great and holy. As for myself, although I am well aware of the case made on the other side, I am greatly distressed at the outrage, whether it be for its gravity or for its novelty, all the more so because close ties link me with a number of those who were responsible for it.[6]

B. I think I begin to see what worries not so much you perhaps as those spiteful critics of other men's virtue whom you believe you ought to satisfy. I divide into three main types those who will rail so vehemently against the seizure of the queen. The first is the most pernicious. To it belong those who minister to tyrannical lusts, who believe that anything is just and honourable which enables them to gratify kings and who measure everything not by its intrinsic worth but by the pleasure it gives their masters. Such men have so enslaved themselves to someone else's passions that they have left themselves no freedom of speech or action. From this school emerged those who most brutally sacrificed an innocent young man, not through personal enmity, but for the pleasure of another and in the hope of profit, preferment and power at court. When those you refer to pretend to grieve for the queen they are not lamenting her misfortunes, but want to ensure their own future safety, and are angry at finding such a great prize for their villainous crime, already devoured in anticipation, snatched from their gullets. [*They seem to me to behave just as foxes usually do (as is related by hunters) who, when they see their lair besieged, start a hare and, while the dogs are chasing it, steal away from danger through the opposite side of the wood.*

M. *I do not understand how this analogy is relevant.*

B. *When Pericles had lavished a large sum of money on the gateway of Minerva and did not see any easy way of rendering an account of it, and was extremely embarrassed by the thought, they say that his stepson Alcibiades advised him to see, rather, how he might avoid rendering any account at all. Eagerly seizing upon the young man's advice, he stirred up the grievous and prolonged Peloponnesian War which, while ensuring that he did not have to render his accounts, destroyed by far the most flourishing of all cities.[7] Likewise, in our own day, a most pernicious civil war broke out in France for the same reason. For when a few seditious men wanted to purchase at the cost of public ruin their own particular impunity and immunity, they preferred, lest they perish alone, to commit everything along with themselves to a different fate.[8] For those who are gnawed by an insistent consciousness of their crimes act rather like cuttle-fish, which stain the water with ink in order to evade the fishermen's nets; fearing for their own skins, they throw the state into confusion as they shamefully and wickedly seek a cloak for their crimes. Do you understand enough so far? Or would you like me to explain the matter in more detail?*

M. *I think I understand enough, so continue what you have begun.*]

[B.] This species of men ought in my opinion to be punished by the severity of the laws and by force of arms rather than by mere words. There are others who are completely devoted to their own interests. These men, in other respects by no means evil, are not troubled by public injustice (as they wish to appear) but by personal injury, and seem to me to need relief rather than the kind of remedy offered by reason or the laws. This leaves the ignorant mob: they are astonished by anything new, usually find fault with it, and think nothing is right unless they themselves either do it or see it done. For they think that any departure from ancestral custom amounts to a departure from justice and equity. Not being influenced by malice, envy or any self-interest, they generally submit to instruction and allow themselves to be weaned away from error, and in most cases they yield to the force of rational argument. In the case of religion, we often find these days, as we have in the past, that hardly anyone is 'so savage that he cannot be tamed if only he lends a patient ear to instruction'.[9]

M. We have certainly found this absolutely true on many occasions.

B. Suppose, then, that you were addressing the mob: if you were to ask the most vociferous and unreasonable among them what they felt about the punishment of Caligula, Nero or Domitian, I think that none of them would be so devoted to the name of king as not to admit that they suffered justly.[10]

M. You may be right. However, these same men will at once exclaim that they are not complaining about the punishment of tyrants, but are angered by the undeserved misfortunes of lawful kings.

B. You see, then, how easily the mob may be appeased?

M. No, you will have to explain in more detail.

B. I shall soon show you. The common people (as you say) approve of the murder of tyrants but are concerned at the misfortunes of kings. Do you not feel, then, that if they clearly understood the difference between a tyrant and a king, they might, in many instances, change their minds?

M. If everyone accepted your point that the killing of tyrants is lawful, it would let us go straight on to the other issues. I see, however, that certain writers, men whose authority is not to be scorned, subject legitimate kings to legal penalties, but nonetheless maintain that tyrants are sacrosanct. A wrong-headed notion, of course, if I am not mistaken, yet they are prepared to fight to the end to protect the authority of tyrants, however extreme and intolerable it may be, as if they were fighting for hearth and home.

B. I too have come across people on several occasions who stubbornly defend that point of view. But we can more conveniently discuss elsewhere whether they are right or wrong. Meanwhile, if you will, let us take for granted our own point of view, on the understanding that, if you do not think it adequately proved later on, you will be free to withdraw your assent to it.[11]

M. On that condition, I have no objection.

B. We shall lay it down, then, that these two, a king and a tyrant, are opposites.

M. Agreed.

B. Then if someone has explained the origin and the reasons for creating kings, and the duties of kings towards their peoples and of peoples towards their kings, you will agree that he has virtually given an explanation which applies conversely to the nature of tyrants?

M. I believe so.

B. And do you not think that, having established a picture of them both, the common people will also understand their own duty towards each of them?

M. It is likely.

B. On the other hand there can exist in things which are very dissimilar but which fall into the same category certain similarities which might easily mislead the unwary?

M. Undoubtedly there can, and particularly that category where the worse person easily passes himself off as the better and aims at nothing other than to impose on the ignorant.

B. Do you have some picture of a king and a tyrant sketched out in your mind? If you do, you will make my task much lighter.

M. I could easily explain what picture I have in mind of each of them, but I am afraid it is rough and shapeless. So rather than engage in a protracted discussion while you refute me I prefer to hear what your views are. You are older and more experienced and not only know the views of others, but have yourself 'observed the customs and the cities of many men'.[12]

B. I shall gladly do what you ask, but I shall explain not so much my own views as those of the ancients. Hence what I say will have greater authority, for it will not be thought up just for the occasion but derived from the opinions of those who, since they have no part in the present controversy, pronounced their conclusions no less clearly than concisely, and without hatred, bias or spite, for which they had no motive.[13] I shall make particular use of the views, not of those who have grown old in seclusion and leisure, but of those who through their virtue and wisdom have distinguished themselves in well-ordered commonwealths both at home and abroad. But before I bring them forward as witnesses, I want to put a few questions to you so that, once we have agreed on certain matters of no little importance, it will not be necessary for me to depart from my line of argument and to linger over explaining or corroborating details which are obvious and almost self-evident.

M. I think that is what we should do, so put whatever question you wish.[14]

*

B. Do you think there was once a time when men lived in huts and even in caves, living a wandering, nomadic existence without laws or settled habitations, and that they gathered together as their fancy took them or some common convenience and advantage inclined them?[15]

M. I believe that is the case, as it accords with the order of nature and is confirmed by almost every historical account of every people. Homer describes how even in the time of the Trojans that kind of wild and uncouth life was lived in Sicily: 'They have no market-places thronged with councils and judges, and have no dwellings but dark caves among the high mountains. Each rules over his own home and wife and children, and no one has time to think with others of the common good.'[16] In these same times Italy is said to have been just as uncivilised and, as these were the most fertile regions in virtually the whole world, it is easy to guess how great a waste and wilderness then existed nearer here.[17]

B. Which do you think more in accordance with nature, that kind of solitary wandering life or the harmonious gatherings and companies of men?

M. Undoubtedly the companies of men which 'expediency herself, virtually the mother of justice and equity', first brought together, bidding them 'to use one common trumpet to give the signal for battle, to be protected by the same walls and enclosed within gates which have a single key.'[18]

B. What? Do you think expediency was the first and greatest means of uniting men?

M. Of course, for I have heard from the most learned men that it was for the sake of men that men were created.[19]

B. Certainly, some people believe that expediency has great influence in establishing and maintaining human society. But if I am not mistaken, there is a much more ancient motive for men associating together and a much earlier and more sacred bond of fellowship between them. After all, if each person were to pursue his own private advantage, surely that self-same expediency would break up human society rather than unite it.

M. That may possibly be true. But I am anxious to hear what other source of human fellowship there might be.

B. Not only men but also the more tame among other creatures have implanted within them a certain force of nature such that, even when the attractions of expediency are absent, they nevertheless willingly assemble together with creatures of their own kind. The other animals are not relevant to our present discussion; but we certainly see this force so deeply imprinted in man by nature that, were someone to have in abundance all those things which are meant to ensure his safety or to please and delight his soul, he would still think his life disagreeable without human intercourse. Indeed even those whose thirst for knowledge and eager pursuit of truth led them to withdraw from the throng and retire to secluded retreats could not bear the unremitting effort of mind for very long or, when they relaxed their concentration, remain confined in solitude. Instead they gladly shared the results of their solitary studies and contributed the fruits of their labour for all to enjoy, as if they had been toiling for the common good. If someone is completely captivated by solitude, and flees and avoids the company of other men, I think it is the result of a diseased mind rather than a natural force, as we have heard, for example, of Timon the Athenian, and of Bellerophon the Corinthian 'who wandered alone and sad on the Elaean shores, eating his heart out and avoiding the tracks of men.'[20]

M. I do not altogether disagree with you here. But you have used one term – nature – which I often employ more from force of habit than because I understand it, while others apply it in such different senses and to so many things that I am in some doubt as to how exactly I should apply it.

B. For the moment, I really want it understood as nothing other than a light divinely shed upon our minds. For when God formed 'this creature which is more holy and more capable of nobility of thought

... and which could be master of all others', [21] He not only gave eyes to man's body as guides to aid him in avoiding what was harmful to his condition and in seeking what was advantageous, but He also set a kind of light before his soul by which he could distinguish base from noble things. Some call this power nature, others call it the law of nature. For my part, I think it is of divine origin, and I am quite convinced that 'nature never says one thing and wisdom another'. [22] Besides, God gave us a kind of summary which encapsulates His whole law in a few words, namely, that we should love Him sincerely and our neighbours as ourselves. [23] All the books of Holy Scripture which are concerned with shaping human behaviour [*and the commentaries of lawyers and philosophers which are in any way useful to mankind*] are no more than an exposition of this law.

M. You think, then, that it was not some orator or lawyer who assembled men together, but that the author of human society was God Himself. [24]

B. Exactly so; for like Cicero, I think there is nothing on earth more pleasing to the supreme God who rules this world than those communities of men bound by the law which are called commonwealths. [25] The various parts of these commonwealths want to be linked together in the same way as all the limbs of the human body work together, in order to balance reciprocal duties, to labour for the common good, to ward off common dangers, to provide for mutual benefits, and, by sharing these things, to secure the goodwill of all towards all.

M. You are convinced, then, that it was not expediency but that law of God implanted in us from the beginning of the world that was the more venerable and divine reason why men came together in a single community.

B. Certainly, I do not see expediency as the mother of justice and equity, as some would have it, but rather as their handmaiden and one of the guardians of a well-ordered commonwealth.

M. Here too I readily agree with you.

B. Now just as in our bodies, composed as they are of conflicting elements, there arise diseases, that is certain internal disorders and disturbances, so the same applies to these larger bodies which we call commonwealths. For they are composed of men of diverse and in a sense opposing sorts, ranks, conditions and characters – of men, indeed, who cannot 'last out even an hour approving the same things'[26] – and must of necessity speedily disintegrate and perish unless someone is employed, in the same way as a doctor, to relieve disturbances. Through a balanced and wholesome regimen, he can strengthen the weaker parts with poultices, curb excessive humours, and take such care of the individual limbs that the feebler parts do not waste away from lack of nourishment and the stronger do not grow to excess.[27]

M. That is clearly essential.

B. What name shall we give to the man who performs this function in the body politic?

M. I am not greatly troubled over the name, for no matter what he is called I judge him to be a most outstanding man who clearly has a very close resemblance to God.[28] In this respect our ancestors in their wisdom seem to me to have shown great foresight, for they took something highly attractive in itself and embellished it with a name of the greatest distinction. For you mean, I imagine, a king, a term whose power is such that it conjures up almost before our very eyes something that is in itself of the highest value and excellence.

B. You are right, for that is the term by which we address God. We have no more venerable word by which to express the pre-eminence of His incomparable nature, nor one which more aptly describes His fatherly love and care for us. I need scarcely mention other terms which we use figuratively to describe the function of a king, father Aeneas, for example, Agamemnon shepherd of the people, likewise leader, prince, helmsman.[29] The underlying meaning of all these terms is such as to show that kings are created, not for themselves, but for the people.[30] But now that we have reached a satisfactory agreement over the name, let us, if you will, discuss his function, continuing along the same path as we took from the start.

M. What was that, tell me?

B. Do you remember what was said a little earlier, that there appears to be a close similarity between a commonwealth and the human body, between civil disturbances and diseases, between a king and a doctor? Once, therefore, we have understood the nature of a doctor's function, we shall not be far, I think, from grasping the function of a king.[31]

M. It may be so, for the other things you mentioned seemed to me very similar – almost blood-brothers.

B. Do not expect me to examine every tiny detail here. Time is too short for that, and the subject itself does not require it. But if they are similar to each other in the most important points, you can easily supply the other details for yourself.

M. By all means, go on as you have been doing.

B. It seems to me that a doctor and a king both have the same end in view.

M. What is that, tell me?

B. The health of the body which each of them is called upon to treat.

M. I understand, for, as far as circumstances permit, one of them keeps the human body in a healthy state and restores it to proper health when it is affected by disease, while the other does the same for the body politic.

B. You are right. Each of them has a double duty: on the one hand, to preserve good health, and on the other, to restore it when it has been undermined by disease.

M. I agree.

B. For the diseases are similar in each case.

M. So it seems.

B. For both are harmed by an excess of harmful elements and a lack of those that are good for them. Each, moreover, is treated in almost the same way, namely, by nourishment and gentle care when it is weak and emaciated, or, when it is full and suffering from excess, by providing relief through the removal of superfluous matter, and by the use of moderate exercise.

M. Quite so. Yet there seems to be a difference in that in the one case it is humours and in the other habits which have to be restored to a proper balance.

B. You grasp the point. For the body politic, like the physical body, has its own special equilibrium which, I think, we can most properly call justice. It is justice that oversees the individual parts and ensures that they continue to fulfil their functions; it removes excess, sometimes by blood-letting, sometimes by expelling harmful elements, as if by a purgative; sometimes it arouses despondent and fearful minds, and comforts those lacking in confidence, restoring the whole body to that balance which I mentioned. Once restored, justice exercises the body with appropriate labours and, by prescribing a due measure of work and leisure, preserves as far as possible the health which has been regained.

M. I readily grant the rest of what you say, but you base the harmony of the body politic on justice when, by its very name and profession, temperance seems to claim that role in its own right.

B. I do not think it matters greatly to which of them you assign this honour. For just as all the virtues whose effect is seen in action are based on some degree of moderation and equability, so they are connected together and inter-related in such a way that all seem to have a single function, that is, the restraint of the passions.[32] In whatever circumstances it operates, it does not greatly matter which name you use, although that moderation which is concerned with public affairs and with men's dealings with one another seems to me to be most aptly comprehended under the name of justice.

M. I am very ready to agree with you in this.

B. Now in the making of a king, I think the ancients followed the principle that if there was someone of outstanding distinction among the citizenry who seemed to surpass all the others in justice and prudence they voluntarily conferred the kingship upon him, as is said to happen in beehives.[33]

M. That is a plausible account of what happened.

B. But what if no single person such as we have described could be found in the commonwealth?

M. By that law of nature which we mentioned earlier an equal neither can nor should assume authority over his equals. For by nature it is just, I think, that those who are equal in all other respects should be equal by turns in ruling and obeying.[34]

B. What if a people, weary of annual electioneering,[35] want to elect as king some individual who does not possess absolutely every kingly virtue but is outstanding either for his nobility, his wealth or his achievements in war? Shall we not consider him a king established by the best of titles?

M. The very best. For the people have the right to bestow authority on whomever they wish.

B. What if we call in to treat diseases a man who is shrewd yet does not possess exceptional skill in the art? Shall we regard him as a doctor the moment he has been elected by everyone?

M. Not at all. For it is not votes, but learning and experience of many arts which make someone a doctor.

B. What about the practitioners of the other arts?

M. In my opinion the same principle applies to them all.

B. Do you think that there is a kind of art of ruling?

M. Of course I do.

B. Can you explain why you believe so?

M. I think I can, namely, the one which is usually given in the case of the other arts.

B. What do you mean?

M. All the arts had their origins in experience. For while the majority of men set about things casually and without thought, others through practice and habit pursued the same activities more skilfully. When they had noted favourable and unfavourable results and weighed up their causes, men of intelligence organised a system of rules and gave it the name of art.[36]

B. Is it possible, then, by a similar process of observation, to define an art of government, as with the art of medicine?

M. I think it is possible.

B. On what rules will it be based?

M. I do not have an answer to hand.

B. What if we investigate this by comparing it with the other arts?

M. In what way?

B. Like this. There are certain rules of grammar as of medicine and husbandry.

M. I understand.

B. Should we not call these rules of grammar and medicine arts and laws? And similarly in other cases?

M. That seems exactly right.

B. What about civil laws? Do they not seem to you to amount to rules of the art of ruling?

M. Yes, they do.

B. It is fitting, therefore, that anyone who wants to be considered a king should understand these laws.

M. So it seems.

B. What if he does not understand them? Do you think he should be called a king, even if the people have decreed that he should rule?

M. Here you make me hesitate. If I want to be consistent with our earlier discussion, the votes of the people can no more make a king than they can make any other artist.

B. What do you believe we should do at this point? For unless we have a king chosen by election, I am afraid we are not going to have any legitimate ruler at all.

M. That is the very thing I am afraid of as well.

B. Would you like us, then, to examine more closely what we said just now when comparing the various arts?

M. Yes, if that is what you wish.

B. We gave the name of laws to the rules adhered to by the practitioners of the individual arts, did we not?

M. Yes, we did.

B. But I am afraid we did so without sufficient care.

M. Why?

B. Because it seems absurd that someone should be master of any art, but not be an artist.

M. Yes, that would be absurd.

B. But anyone who discharges the function of an art, we consider an artist, whether he does it naturally or by ceaseless and consistent judgement and skill.

M. I think so.

B. Whoever, therefore, possesses this judgement or skill in doing anything correctly, we shall call an artist, provided he acquired his skill by practice.

M. More so than someone else who merely knows the rules but lacks experience and practice.

B. We are not, then, to regard the rules themselves as the art?

M. Not at all; they are a kind of semblance or, more properly, the shadow of the art.

B. So what is that skill in governing commonwealths which we call the art or science of politics?

M. You seem to me to want to say prudence, from which as from a fountain all laws must be drawn and derived if they are to have value for the preservation of human society.

B. You have hit the nail on the head. If this quality could be found in complete and perfect form in anyone, we would call him a king by nature, not men's votes, and we would hand over to him unrestricted power in all matters; but if we cannot find such a person, we shall give the name of king to the man who comes closest to that surpassing excellence of nature, cherishing in him a certain semblance of the true king.[37]

M. Let us give him that name if you will.

B. And since we fear that he may not be strong enough to combat his emotions, which can and usually do divert men from the truth, we shall give him the law as a colleague or rather as a curb on his passions.

M. You do not think, then, that the king ought to possess complete power over all matters?

B. Not at all. For I recall that he is not only a king but a human being as well, erring in many things through ignorance, often transgressing of his own will, often almost against his will, since he is a creature readily changing with every breath of popularity or hatred. This natural vice is usually only intensified in a magistrate, so much so that here especially I find that famous aphorism of comedy to be true, that 'everyone becomes worse if he is allowed to do as he pleases'.[38] That is why men of the greatest wisdom have proposed that the law should be yoked to the king to show him the way when he does not know it or to lead him back to it when he wanders from it. From these remarks, I think, you can see, as in a relief, what I believe to be the function of a true king.

M. You have satisfied me completely on the reason for creating kings, and on their name and function, though I will not object if you want to add anything. In truth, even though my mind hurries on towards the topics which appear to remain, there was one aspect of your reasoning which perturbed me somewhat and which I do not think should be passed over in silence, namely, that you seem a little unfair to kings. This is precisely the suspicion I have frequently had of you before, since I have often heard you praising the republics of antiquity and the Venetian commonwealth in extravagant terms.[39]

B. You have not understood my views on this correctly. For I admire the Romans, the Massilians, the Venetians and any others for whom the authority of the laws was more powerful than that of men, not so much for their different method of administering the commonwealth as for their justice.[40] I do not think it matters much whether the person who rules is called king, doge, emperor or consul, provided it is remembered that he is placed in office for the sake of maintaining justice. So long as the authority is lawful, there is no need for us to argue about its name. The man whom we call doge of the Venetians is nothing other than a lawful king. Likewise, the first consuls retained not only the insignia of kings but also their authority. The only difference was that there was not one ruler but two (you are aware that this was also the custom with the Spartan kings, who ruled for life[41]), and that they were appointed not for life but for a year.[42] You should always bear in mind, then, what we said at the beginning, that kings were first established in order to maintain justice. If they had remembered this, they could have retained their authority permanently as they had first received it, that is, free and unrestrained by laws.[43] But (as with all things human) the state of affairs deteriorated badly and political authority, originally established in the public interest, turned into an overbearing tyranny. When the lust of kings served in place of law and men who wielded unlimited and uncontrolled power showed no self-restraint but gave free rein to favouritism, hatred and self-interest, the insolence of kings made laws a necessity. This was the reason, then, why laws were devised by peoples, and why in administering justice kings were compelled to exercise, not their own arbitrary wills, but the authority over the people which the people had granted them. For the people had learned from long experience that it was better to entrust their liberty to laws than to kings; while many motives could deflect kings from the truth, the laws maintained a single, unchanging course, deaf to entreaties and to threats.[44] Kings, therefore, although free in all other respects, have this one limit set to their authority, that their speech and actions should conform to the precepts of the law and that they should apportion rewards and punishments, the strongest bonds of human society, according to its sanctions. In short, in the words of the greatest teacher of the art of governing a commonwealth, the king should be 'the law speaking' and the law 'a silent king'.[45]

M. Right from the beginning you praised kings so warmly that you made their majesty almost sacred and holy. But now, as if struck with remorse, you restrict them to a kind of close confinement, and casting them, as it were, into the prison of the laws, you do not even allow them free speech. You have made me abandon the high hopes I had, for I expected that either of your own accord or at my prompting you would during your discourse restore to its proper brilliance something which is (in the words of the most renowned of historians) 'most illustrious among gods and men';[46] instead you have reduced it to subjection and robbed it of all distinction and, by confining it behind bars, made what was the highest office in the world so contemptible that no one in his right mind would want it. For who of sound mind would not prefer to remain a private citizen of modest means rather than arrange the whole course of his life according to other men's rules, facing endless difficulties, concentrating on the concerns of others and neglecting his own? If government on these terms were adopted universally, I am afraid there would be a greater scarcity of kings than there was of bishops when our religion was in its first infancy. If kings are to be judged by this standard, I am not surprised that formerly men were fetched from the pastures and the plough to accept such a distinguished honour.[47]

B. Consider, I beg you, how wrong you are in thinking that it was not for the enjoyment of justice but for pleasure that kings were sought by peoples and nations, and in believing that there is no honour in a position where riches and pleasures do not abound.[48] Consider how much you detract from the dignity of kings in this matter. To let you understand this more easily, compare the likeness you look for in our description of a king with one of those kings whom you have seen dressed up like a child's doll and, puffed up with pride, paraded in empty pomp surrounded by a vast retinue. Compare, I say, one of these kings with those who were famous long ago, whose memory even now lives and flourishes and is honoured by posterity. Such kings certainly were of the kind I have just described. Have you ever heard the story of the old woman who asked Philip of Macedon to listen to her case? When he replied that he did not have the time to spare, she rejoined, 'Then you should not be a king'.[49] Have you heard, I ask you, that when the king, victor in so many wars, conqueror of so many peoples, was reminded of his duty by a poor old woman, he obeyed her and acknowledged what the office of a king entailed? Compare this Philip, then, not merely with the greatest kings there are in Europe today but with the memory of all past times: you will certainly not find his match in prudence, courage and the endurance of hardships, and few equals in the extent of his dominion. If I were to mention Agesilaus, Leonidas and all the other Spartan kings – and what men they were! – I would appear to be offering hackneyed examples.[50] Yet there is one remark of a Spartan girl, Gorgo, the daughter of Cleomenes, which I cannot pass over in silence. When she saw a servant pulling off an Asiatic guest's slippers, she ran to her father and called out, 'Father, our guest has no hands.' From the girl's remark you can easily judge the general character of Spartan discipline as well as the domestic habits of their kings.[51] Those who underwent this rustic but manly training achieved great things, whatever value you place on them; but those trained under the Asiatic system lost through luxury and indolence the extensive kingdoms handed down by their ancestors. But leaving aside the ancients, not so very long ago the Galicians had such a person in Pelagius, the first man to weaken the power of the Saracens in Spain; although at his home 'hearth and household gods, herds and their masters all sheltered together',[52] nevertheless the Spanish kings were so far from being ashamed of him that they think it their greatest glory to be descended from him.[53]

However, since this topic requires a longer discussion, let us go back to the point where we digressed. For, as promised, I want to show you as soon as possible that this form of kingship was not devised by me, but that the same view has been held by men of the greatest renown throughout history, and I will show you briefly the sources from which I have drawn it. Cicero's books entitled *On Duties* are by general consent accorded the highest praise. From the second book come these exact words:

It seems to me that not only among the Medes (as Herodotus claims[54]) but also among our own ancestors men of the highest character were once upon a time appointed kings in order that justice might be enjoyed. Since in the beginning the masses were oppressed by those who had greater wealth, they turned for protection to some individual of outstanding integrity who, while protecting the weak from wrong, would, by establishing equity, restrain high and low alike by equal law. Laws and kings were established for the same reason. For the law always aims at justice, otherwise it would not be the law. If the people obtained this from a single just and good man, they were content; when they did not, laws were invented which always spoke to everyone with one and the same voice. So this at least is clear, that those usually chosen to govern were those whose reputation for justice was highest among the masses. If in addition they were considered to be prudent, there was nothing which men thought they could not achieve under their leadership.[55]

You see from these words, I think, what Cicero considers the reason for striving after both kings and laws. Here I might also praise Xenophon as my witness and supporter, a man renowned as much for achievements in war as for the study of philosophy, but I know he is so familiar to you that you are acquainted with all his views.[56] As for Plato and Aristotle, although I am well aware how highly you value them, I leave them aside for the moment; for I prefer to summon to my aid distinguished men from active politics rather than from the scholar's retreat.[57] Still less did I think I should bring before you the Stoic king such as Seneca describes in his *Thyestes*, not so much because his portrait of the true king is not perfect as because that model of a good prince can be more readily imagined in the mind than hoped for some day.[58] But also, to avoid giving grounds for cavilling over those I have cited, I have not put before you kings from the Scythian desert who skinned their own horses or carried on some other work much more repugnant to our ways;[59] instead I have cited examples from the heart of Greece, men who, in those very times when the Greeks were most distinguished in all the liberal arts, ruled over the greatest nations and well-regulated commonwealths, and did so in such a way that as in life they enjoyed the greatest honour among their own people so in death they bequeathed an illustrious memory to posterity.[60]

M. If you ask me what I think now, I hardly dare admit my uncertainty or timidity or whatever other name you please to give to that fault. For every time I read the views you have just quoted expressed by the finest writers of histories, or hear them commended by men of great wisdom whose authority I would not dare to disregard, and approved by all good men, they seem to me to be not only true, proper and sound, but also persuasive and noble. On the other hand, every time I turn my eyes upon the refinements and elegance of our own day, those times of old seem to have been pure and upright but uncouth and not yet adequately polished. But perhaps we shall have leisure to deal with this on another occasion; for the present, if you will, go on with what you have begun.

B. Would you like us, then, to summarise briefly what has been said? In this way we can best understand what has been omitted and most easily re-examine any point conceded unthinkingly.

M. Yes, that will be best.

B. First of all, then, we agreed that men were made by nature for living together in society.

M. That was agreed.

B. Also that as guardian of that society a king was chosen, an outstanding man of the highest virtue.

M. That is so.

B. And just as the disagreements of men among themselves made it necessary to create a king, so the injuries done by kings to their subjects were the reason for our needing laws.

M. Yes.

B. We decided, then, that the laws provide a pattern for the art of kingship, just as the rules of medicine provide one for the medical art.

M. Yes.

B. It seems safer (since in neither case did we assume that he had unique and exact skill in his art) that each should work in accordance with the rules of his art rather than haphazardly.

M. Yes, that is safer.

B. Now the rules of medicine did not seem to be of one kind.

M. What do you mean?

B. Some are meant to protect health, others to restore it.

M. Quite right.

B. What about the art of kingship?

M. There are just as many types, I imagine.

B. It seems, then, that the next point we should consider is whether you think that doctors can have such a precise understanding of all diseases and their remedies that nothing further could be required for their treatment?

M. Not at all, for in almost every age many new types of disease break out, and likewise almost every year new remedies are either devised by men's diligence or brought from distant parts.

B. What about the laws of commonwealths?

M. Yes, the same principle seems to apply to them.

B. So the rules of their art handed down in writing do not enable either doctors or kings to avoid or to cure all diseases.

M. I do not think that is possible.

B. Should we investigate, then, what are the topics on which laws can be enacted in commonwealths, and which topics cannot be covered by laws?

M. That will be worth doing.

*

B. It seems to me that there are numerous matters of great importance which cannot be covered by any laws. First, everything which falls under the heading of deliberation about the future.

M. Yes, everything of that kind.

B. Next, many past events, such as those in which the truth is sought by conjecture, confirmed by testimony or extracted by torture.

M. Of course.

B. What, then, will be the role of the king in settling these questions?

M. I do not think there is any need for long discussion here, since far from claiming supreme power for themselves in matters which are concerned with taking thought for the future, kings voluntarily summon wiser men to their council.

B. What about cases which are decided by arguments or proved by witnesses, such as charges of murder, adultery or poisoning?

M. Matters of that kind are examined and brought to light by the skill and shrewdness of advocates, and I observe that they are generally left to the verdict of judges.

B. And perhaps rightly. For if a king should want to hear the private cases of individual subjects, when will he have time to think about war and peace and about those measures which preserve and maintain the safety of the commonwealth? In fact when will he be allowed to rest?

M. I would not wish the hearing of every question to be referred to the king alone; for one man could not deal with each case of every subject, if it were brought before him. So I very much like that advice, no less wise than essential, which Moses' father-in-law gave him, that the burden of administering justice should be shared among many. But I shall not speak further of this, since the story is known to everyone.[61]

B. But even these judges will, I imagine, pronounce judgement in accordance with what is prescribed in the laws.

M. They will indeed. Yet it seems to me that there are only a few matters for which the laws can make provision compared with those for which they cannot provide.

B. There is in addition another problem of no less difficulty, for not all matters concerning which laws are passed can be covered by definite provisions.

M. How so?

B. Lawyers, who value their art very highly and who want to be regarded as the priests of justice,[62] acknowledge the number of cases to be so great that it can seem almost infinite, and they say that every day new crimes appear in commonwealths like sores of different kinds. What will the law-maker, who shapes the laws in the light of the present and the past, accomplish in these circumstances?

M. Not much, unless he is somebody superhuman.

B. And there is one more difficulty, and no small one at that, for human affairs are so uncertain that hardly any art can lay down fixed and invariable rules to cover all cases.[63]

M. Nothing could be more true.

B. The safer course, then, seems to be to entrust the health of a patient to an experienced physician and the welfare of a commonwealth to a king. For a doctor, by venturing beyond the rules of his art, will often cure a sick man, either with his consent or sometimes against his will, and the king can impose a new yet beneficial law on his subjects either by persuasion or even against their will.[64]

M. I can see nothing to prevent him.

B. But when either of them acts in this way, surely he does not seem to you to be going against the law appropriate to him?

M. It seems to me that each is acting in accordance with his art. For earlier we laid it down that an art does not consist of rules but is a mental power which the artist is accustomed to use in handling the subject-matter of his art. But I am glad (assuming that you are speaking sincerely) that you have been compelled, as it were, by the interdict of Truth herself, to restore the king to the position from which he had been deposed by force.

B. Wait a moment – you have not heard everything yet. There is another disadvantage in the supreme authority of the laws. For like some obstinate and ignorant task-master, the law thinks nothing right except what it commands itself. Before a king, one can plead weakness or rashness, and there is room for pardoning someone detected in an offence; but the law is deaf, unfeeling and inexorable.[65] The young man blames the unsteadiness of his age, the woman the weakness of her sex, another poverty, drink, or friends. What does the law reply to these pleas? 'Go, lictor, bind his hands, cover his head, flog him and hang him from the gallows.'[66] You are not unaware how dangerous it can be, among so much human frailty, to rest your hope of safety on innocence alone.

M. Without doubt, the situation you speak of is full of danger.

B. Yes, I see that some people are considerably alarmed whenever it comes to mind.

M. Considerably – you are right about that.

B. So when I reflect more closely on what was assumed by us earlier, I am afraid that in this respect the comparison between a doctor and a king seems to have been introduced inappropriately.

M. In what respect?

B. When we set them both free from enslavement to rules and gave them almost unrestricted power to prescribe treatment.

M. What particularly offends you about this?

B. Listen and you can judge for yourself. We postulated two reasons why it is not in the interest of peoples that kings be unbound by the laws, namely love and hate, which lead the minds of men astray when they are administering justice. In the case of a doctor, indeed, there is no need to fear that he will err through love, since he may even hope for a reward from the patient once his health has been restored; and if the patient realises that his doctor is being incited by entreaties, promises and money to endanger his life, he will be free to summon another doctor, or, if another is not available, I think it is safer for him to seek a remedy in books, deaf though they may be, rather than from a corrupt physician.[67] As we were complaining about the inhumanity of the laws, however, let us see whether we are being altogether consistent with ourselves.

M. In what way?

B. We agreed that the ideal king, the kind we can see more clearly in the mind than with our eyes, ought not to be constrained by any laws.

M. Exactly.

B. Why was that?

M. I imagine it was because, according to Paul, he was to be a law to himself and to others, as one whose life expresses what is commanded by the laws.[68]

B. You are right, and, what may surprise you more, under nature's guidance, Aristotle had seen this very point some centuries before Paul.[69] I mention this to let you see more clearly what was proved earlier, namely, that the voice of God and of nature is the same.[70] But to proceed with our purpose, what shall we say was in the minds of those who first enacted laws?

M. Justice, I imagine, as has already been said.

B. I am not asking at present what objective they had in mind, but rather what model they had set before themselves.

M. Although I think I understand what you mean, I should like you to explain. Then if I have it right, you can confirm my judgement; if not, you can correct my mistake.

B. You know, I imagine, what power the mind has over the body.

M. I think so.

B. You are also not unaware that, whenever we do something with deliberation, there is a certain likeness of it in our minds beforehand, and one which is much more perfect than the works which even the finest artists fashion and, as it were, create on the basis of that model.

M. Yes, I often find this myself both in speaking and writing, and I feel that my words fail to match what is in my mind no less than my thoughts fail to match the objects themselves. Shut up in this dark and confused prison of the body, our minds cannot perceive the fine detail of everything.[71] Likewise, when mental pictures of things take shape in our minds, we cannot convey them to others in speech in such a way that they are not greatly inferior to those which our understanding has formed for itself.

B. Then what shall we say was in the minds of those who enacted laws?

M. I think I am close to understanding what you mean: namely, that they had in view an image of that ideal king and, as closely as they could, they had created a model, not of his physical body, but of his thoughts, and that they wanted to have as their laws whatever that ideal king would have considered good and just.

B. You understand me correctly – that is exactly what I meant. Now I should like you to consider what qualities we have assigned to the ideal king from the beginning. Did we not make him resolute against hatred, love, anger, envy and all other disturbances of the mind?

M. We certainly imagined him like that, or believed him actually to have existed among those men of old.

B. The laws, then, seem to have been made in his image?

M. The resemblance could not be closer.

B. A good king, therefore, is no less hard and unyielding than a good law.

M. Just as hard. However, although I neither can nor should wish to change either of them, I should like, if I may, to soften both of them a little.

B. Yet God does not wish us to take pity even on the poor in administering justice, but commands us to consider only what is right and just and to pronounce judgement in accordance with that alone.[72]

M. I acknowledge the correctness of that view, and am 'vanquished by the truth'.[73] Since it is not permitted, then, to exempt the king from the laws, kindly tell me who in the world will be the law-maker whom we will give the king as a sort of schoolmaster?[74]

B. Whom do you think most able to fulfil this function?

M. If you ask me, I think the king himself. For generally in the other arts we see the artists themselves handing down the rules of their art, which they use, like a set of notes, to refresh their own memories and to remind others of their duty.

B. I, on the other hand, see no difference between leaving the king free and unbound by the laws and granting him the power to enact them. For no one will voluntarily put fetters on himself. Indeed, I wonder if it is not better to leave the king unrestrained than to put him in chains which, in so far as he can lay them aside whenever he wishes, will serve no purpose.

M. But in entrusting the government of the kingdom to laws rather than to kings, you must beware, I beg you, not to subject this man, whom in name you have made a king, to a tyrant who can 'hold him down by his authority and curb him with chains and prison-bars'; and only stop short of loading him with fetters and sending him to work on the land or to serve in the mill.[75]

B. Fine words! I am not imposing anyone as master over him, but I want the people, who have granted him authority over themselves, to be allowed to dictate to him the extent of his authority, and I require him to exercise as a king only such right as the people have granted him over them. Nor do I wish these laws to be imposed by force, as you interpret it. Rather I believe that, after consultation with the king in council, a decision should be taken in common in matters which affect the common good of all.

M. Then you want to grant this function to the people?

B. Yes, to the people, unless perhaps you think otherwise.

M. Nothing, it seems to me, could be less just.

B. Why is that?

M. You are familiar with the phrase 'the many-headed monster'.[76] You know, I think, how rash and fickle the people are.

B. I have never thought that this task should be left to the judgement of the people as a whole. Rather, as is roughly our own practice, selected men from all estates should meet with the king in council; then, once a 'preliminary resolution' has been drawn up by them, it should be referred to the judgement of the people.[77]

M. I quite understand your suggestion, but you seem to me to achieve nothing by this careful safeguard. You do not wish the king to be exempt from the laws. Why not? It is, in my view, because within man two extremely savage monsters, lust and anger, wage ceaseless war with reason:[78] so laws were demanded which would curb their licentiousness and bring them back, when they ran to excess, to respect for lawful authority. But what of those counsellors of yours furnished from the ranks of the people? Are they themselves not plagued by that same internal war? Are they too not tormented by the same evils as afflict the king? Thus the more helpers you attach to the king as assessors, the greater will be the number of fools, and you can imagine what is to be expected from that.

B. But my expectations are far from what you imagine, and I shall tell you why. Firstly, it is not altogether true, as you believe, that nothing is gained by summoning a large number of people together, among whom perhaps no one will possess outstanding wisdom.[79] For not only do the many see and understand more than any one of them on his own, but they see more even than a single individual who surpasses each of them in intelligence and good sense. As a general rule, a multitude of people is a better judge of all affairs than an individual. Individuals have certain small portions of virtue which, when brought together, form a single outstanding virtue. This can be clearly seen in the drugs used by doctors, and especially in that antidote which they call *Mithridate*.[80] In it numerous ingredients harmful in themselves produce, when mixed together, an effective remedy for poisons. Likewise in men, some are handicapped by slowness and indecision, others by precipitate rashness; but when these qualities are combined in a large group of men they produce a certain mean and that moderation which we seek in every kind of virtue.[81]

M. Suppose that, as you wish, it were in the power of the people to propose and pass laws, and suppose that kings were, so to speak, the door-keepers of the record-offices. But when the laws appear to conflict with one another or make provisions which are not distinct or clear enough, will you want there to be no part for the king to play, especially since, if you wish to decide everything by written law, many absurdities must inevitably result? To use a very trite example, there is that law which is endlessly repeated in the schools: 'If a foreigner mounts the wall, let him be put to death.' What can be more absurd than that the man who has championed the public safety, who has flung the enemy down as they climbed the wall, should himself be hurried off to execution as if he had acted like an enemy?[82]

B. Nothing could be more absurd.

M. Do you approve, then, of that old saying: 'The more law, the more injustice'?[83]

B. Yes, I do.

M. If a question of this kind were to come to court, a lenient interpreter is needed who would not allow laws enacted for the benefit of everyone to prove ruinous to good men innocent of any crime.

B. You are right, and if you have been observant enough, you will have seen that my sole aim throughout this discussion has been to make sacrosanct and inviolable that Ciceronian maxim: 'Let the welfare of the people be the supreme law.'[84] If, then, a case comes to court of such a kind that there is no uncertainty over what is good and just, the king's role will be to ensure that the law is applied according to that rule which I have just mentioned. But you seem to me to demand more in the name of kings than even the most imperious of them claim for themselves. You know that it is usual to refer to judges this kind of case, where the law seems to say one thing and the law-maker to have intended another, just as we refer those cases which arise from ambiguity in the law or from disagreement between laws. Hence it is that advocates engage in the most vehement disputes in court over these matters and the rules of the rhetoricians are most scrupulously handed down.[85]

M. I know that it is as you say. But in this case it seems to me that no less harm is done by the laws than by kings. I think it is better for a legal action to be decided at once according to the verdict of one good man than for clever men, and sometimes sly old lags, to be given the power to obscure rather than to interpret the laws. For in so far as advocates compete not merely to win their clients' cases but to gain renown for their own talent, litigation increases and what is right and lawful, just and unjust, is put at risk; and what we deny to the king we permit to men of lower rank who are generally more devoted to litigation than to the truth.

B. You seem to me to have forgotten what we recently agreed.

M. What was that?

B. The ideal king such as we described at the beginning was to be granted such complete freedom that laws would be unnecessary. But when that office is held by one of the ordinary people, who is not greatly superior to others or is perhaps inferior to some of them, we agreed that that kind of unrestrained licence, exempt from the laws, is dangerous.

M. But what has this to do with the interpretation of the laws?

B. A great deal. Or perhaps you have not noticed that in different words we have restored to the king that unlimited and uncontrolled power which earlier we denied him – namely, the power to turn everything upside down as his fancy takes him.

M. If I am doing what you say, it is certainly unintentional.

B. Then I shall put it more clearly to let you understand. When you concede to the king the right to interpret the laws, you grant him such licence that the law need not express what the law-maker intended or what is just and good for all, but what is in the interests of the interpreter, and in applying it to every case he can modify it like a Lesbian rule to his own advantage.[86] During his decemvirate Appius Claudius had passed a most just law that 'in a case concerning free status judgement should be given in favour of a person claiming his freedom'. What could be more clearly put? Yet by his interpretation of it the very person who framed the law rendered it worthless.[87] You see, I presume, how much licence you give the prince by a single line: namely, that the law says what he wills and does not say what he does not will. If we ever allow this, there will be no point in passing good laws to remind a good prince of his duty and to restrain a bad one. In fact, to put it more clearly, it would be better to have no laws at all than that freebooters should enjoy freedom and even honour under the pretext of the law.

M. Do you think that any king would be so shameless as to take absolutely no account of what people say or think of him, or so forgetful of himself and his family as to sink to the depravity of those whom he has himself punished with disgrace, imprisonment, confiscation of property, and even with the severest of all penalties?

B. We should not believe this possible if it had not happened long before now, and to the great harm of the whole world, too.

M. Tell me where you think this has happened?

B. You ask me where? As if every nation throughout Europe had not only seen but actually experienced how much evil has been brought upon mankind – I will not say by the unrestrained power – but by the unbridled licence of the Roman pontiff. No one is unaware how modest and apparently respectable its origins were, and how nothing was less capable of arousing the fears of the unwary. The laws laid down for us in the beginning were not only derived from the deepest mysteries of nature but enacted by God Himself, interpreted by His spirit through the prophets, and finally confirmed by the Son of God, Himself also God, and commended to us by the writings of so many men of the highest esteem, who expressed them in their lives and sealed them with their blood. In the whole of the law no passage has been more carefully commended to us or more clearly expounded than that concerning the office of bishops; and since it is wrong for anyone to add anything to those laws, to repeal them in whole or in part or to make any change in them, nothing remained but interpretation.[88] Claiming this power for himself, the bishop of Rome not only crushed other churches but assumed the most savage tyranny that ever existed. Daring to command the angels as well as men, he deposed Christ altogether – unless it does not amount to deposition if what you wish prevails in heaven, on earth and in hell, whereas what Christ ordained prevails only if you will it.[89] For if the law does not seem to favour you sufficiently, you can so refine it by interpretation that Christ is not merely compelled to speak through your lips but to express your own opinions. Thus when Christ spoke through the lips of the Roman pontiff, Chilperic was replaced by Pippin,[90] and John of Navarre by Ferdinand of Aragon,[91] son fought impiously against father, and subjects against their king. Christ was steeped in poison, and was then forced to become a poisoner Himself in order to remove Henry of Luxembourg by poison.[92]

M. This is not the first time that I have heard these stories, but I am anxious to have the question of the interpretation of the laws more clearly explained.

B. I shall give you one example from which you will easily see how effective this whole procedure is. There is a law, 'A bishop should be the husband of only one wife'.[93] Could anything be clearer or more explicit than this law? But the pope interprets 'one wife' as 'one church', as if that law had been laid down to restrain the avarice of bishops rather than their lust. This interpretation, although nothing to the purpose, nonetheless does contain a view which is highly respectable and upright, except that the same pope spoiled it with another interpretation. So what does this pontiff devise? 'The position varies', he says, 'according to person, motive, place and time. Some bishops are of such nobility that no number of churches can satisfy their pride. Again some churches are too poor to provide a living even for a monk who, recently a beggar, now wears a mitre, if he wishes to maintain the dignity of the episcopal office.'[94] From that sly interpretation of the law the principle was devised that although bishops are declared to have only one church each, others are entrusted to their care, and all are despoiled. The day would be too short if I wanted to catalogue the subterfuges which they devised on a daily basis to counter this single law. However, unworthy alike of the papal office and even of a Christian, their tyranny did not stop there. For such is the nature of all things that when once they have begun to fall headlong they never stop until they plunge to destruction. Would you like me to illustrate this with a famous example? Can you recall any emperor of Roman blood more cruel or vile than C. Caligula?

M. None that I know of.

B. Now what do you think was his vilest deed? I do not mean those which the pontiffs include among 'reserved cases',[95] but in the rest of his life.

M. Nothing comes to mind.

B. What do you think of his inviting his horse Incitatus to dinner, or serving it with golden barley, or appointing it a consul?[96]

M. Utterly vile acts.

B. What about his enrolling it also as his colleague in the priesthood?[97]

M. Do you mean this seriously?

B. Of course I am serious. I am hardly surprised if these seem like fabrications to you. But our own Roman Jupiter has made them believable to posterity – I mean Pope Julius III, who seems to me to have engaged in a contest with that most vile man C. Caligula to decide who was pre-eminent in wickedness.[98]

M. What enormity did he commit?

B. As his colleague in the priesthood he co-opted the keeper of his ape, a fellow almost viler than the vilest of beasts.

M. Perhaps there was another reason for choosing him.

B. Others are mentioned as well, but I have selected the most respectable. Anyway, since the freedom to interpret the law has resulted not just in so much contempt for the priesthood but also in disregard for humanity, be careful not to think it an insignificant power.

M. Yet the ancients do not seem to me to have thought this power of interpretation as momentous as you would like us to imagine. That this was so is evident from the simple fact that the Roman emperors granted it to jurists.[99] This single consideration upsets all that lengthy argument of yours. Not only does it refute what you said about the importance of that power, but it also clearly demonstrates the point which you are trying so hard to avoid, namely, that the power granted to others to give legal rulings was not denied to the emperors themselves if they had wished to exercise that function or their affairs had allowed them.[100]

B. As far as the Roman emperors are concerned, they do not conform to the pattern of kings which we described, for they were placed in authority by their own soldiers without legal formality or regard for the common good. They were chosen by the most evil type of men, and were generally the most wicked among them, or else they themselves forced their way into that position by violence. I do not criticise them for giving the jurists the power to give legal rulings. For although, as I said earlier, it is a most important power, it is safer to entrust it to those who cannot use it as an instrument of tyranny. Moreover, it was entrusted to a number of men who were held to their duty by mutual respect, so that if they had deviated from what was right they would have been refuted by the ruling of the others. Even if they had conspired together dishonestly there remained the protection offered by the judge, who was not compelled to treat the jurist's ruling as legally binding.[101] There remained also the emperor, who could exact penalties for the violation of the laws. Since they were held in check by so many fetters, and feared a greater penalty than the reward their fraud might bring them, you see, I think, that no very great danger was to be feared from men of that kind.

M. Have you anything more to say about the king?

B. First of all, let us, if you will, make a brief summary of what has been said. This will let us see more easily if anything has been overlooked.

M. I believe that is what we should do.

B. We seemed to be well enough agreed about the origin and the reason for creating kings and laws, but not as regards the law-maker.

In the end, however, you seemed to me to have given your assent, albeit somewhat reluctantly, but yielding to the sheer force of truth.

M. Yes, despite my strenuous advocacy, you have deprived the king of the power not only to enact laws but even to interpret them. I am afraid that if this comes out I may at some time be convicted of collusion, so easily have I allowed you to tear from my grasp a case which seemed sound when we began.[102]

B. Do not be discouraged. If anyone accuses you of collusion I promise to defend you for nothing.

M. Perhaps we shall soon put that to the test.

B. There also seemed to us to be many types of business which cannot be covered by any laws. Without objection from the king we referred some of these to the ordinary judges and some to a council.

M. I remember that. And do you know what occurred to me when you were doing so?

B. How can I unless you tell me?

M. You seemed to me to fashion kings rather like the stone statuettes on the capitals of columns, which seem to strain as if they were supporting the whole structure, when in fact they carry no greater load than any other stone.

B. What, my fine defender of kings! Are you complaining that I impose too light a burden on them, when night and day their one aim is to seek men to share their burden or to relieve them of it altogether? And yet you seem at the same time to be angry that I am bringing them relief from their labours.

M. I too gladly welcome those reinforcements of yours, but I want them to serve, not to command; to point out the way, not to lead the king wherever they please, or rather drag him and push him forward like an engine of war, leaving him no other power save that of agreeing with them. So for a long time now I have been waiting for you to finish your discourse on the king and move on to tyrants or some other topic. For you have confined the king within such narrow bounds that I am afraid that if we spend any more time on the subject you will deprive him of his great wealth and exalted rank and banish him, as it were, to some desert island where he can grow old in want and misery, stripped of all his honours.[103]

B. You were afraid, or so you claim, of being charged with collusion; but my fear is that by bringing a false accusation you will harm the king whom you are trying to defend.[104]   First of all, I do not wish him to be idle, unless you consider that architects are idle. Next you rob him of his excellent assistants and friends, whom I did not assign to him as guards but whom I wanted him to summon for himself to share his task. You remove those friends and surround him with a retinue of good-for-nothings who make him feared by his subjects, and you think he will not inspire dread unless we leave him great power to do harm. I want him to be loved by his subjects, protected not by their fear but by their goodwill, the only weapon which makes kings invincible. If you have no objection, I hope to achieve this in a few words. For I shall lead him from what you call his close confinement into the light and by a single law furnish him with such authority and dignity that you would think him shameless if he desired any more.

M. I am eager to hear what you have in mind.[105]

*

B. Then I shall take up that very topic in order to satisfy your desire as soon as possible. A little earlier we admitted that no law can make such explicit provision for any eventuality that malicious cunning cannot find an opening for fraud. This will perhaps be easier to understand if I cite an example. It was laid down by the laws that fathers should not transmit benefices to their bastards.[106] Yet here, in a matter which seems plain, a fraud was devised: the father appoints someone else in his son's place, and that person hands on the same benefice to the bastard of the former incumbent. Then when an express provision was added to the law that under no circumstances should a son hold a benefice which his father had held at any time, even this proved ineffective: to counter it the priests conspired amongst themselves that each would appoint the other's son in place of his own. When that too was forbidden, the law was evaded by a new type of fraud: a sham litigant is put up against the father who pretends that he has a right to that benefice. While the father skirmishes in mock battle with the fraudulent claimant, the son petitions the Roman pontiff for the benefice should neither of the claimants have a right to it; he wins out over both litigants when they willingly yield to him of their own accord, and so the son obtains his father's benefice through his father's collusion. You see how many types of fraud have been devised concerning only a single law.

M. Yes, I see that.

B. Does it not seem to you that in this respect law-makers do exactly the same as doctors? Physicians try to control outbursts of phlegm or some other harmful fluid by applying a plaster, but the fluid which has been checked in one place seeks a way out in several places at once, and like a hydra, when one head is cut off, many fresh ones spring up in its place.

M. An exact parallel.

B. Just as the physician had to begin by ensuring that he relieved the whole body of harmful fluids once and for all, ought not the doctor of the body politic to act likewise in these circumstances to relieve the entire commonwealth of bad habits?

M. Although what you advise is difficult, I think it is the right type of treatment.

B. And if this were feasible, I believe that few laws would be needed.

M. Exactly so.

B. Does it not seem to you that the man who can provide this treatment is likely to contribute more single-handedly to the public good than all the assemblies of all the estates convened to promulgate laws?

M. Undoubtedly much more. But to quote the comic poet: 'Who will there be here so powerful as to bestow so great a gift?'[107]

B. What if we entrust this role to the king?

M. A fine idea! You handed over to the whole people whatever was simple and straightforward, but you will entrust to the king alone whatever is difficult and unpleasant. As if you were not satisfied, having bound him with chains, to confine him so closely, you now impose upon him a burden so heavy that he will collapse under it.

B. No, it is something he can easily grant, and we are not extorting it, but asking that he let himself be open to entreaty.

M. What entreaties do you mean?

B. That throughout his life he should behave towards his subjects, whom he ought to regard as his children, in the way that he expects fathers to behave towards their children.

M. How is that relevant?

B. This is really the only – certainly the best – antidote to corrupt behaviour. And in case you think that I have made it up, listen to what Claudian says:

> Play the part of a citizen and a father, take thought for everyone, not for yourself, and be influenced not by your own wishes but by those of your people. Whenever you issue a decree for the common good and direct that it should be observed, be the first to submit to it. The people become more ready to comply with what is just and to accept it, when they see its author himself obey it. The example set by a king shapes the world, and edicts have less power than the life of their ruler to influence men's feelings. The fickle masses always alter with the prince.[108]

Do not think that the poet, possessed of the highest intelligence and learning, was wrong to believe this idea to have so much power vested in it. For the common people are so disposed to imitate those from whom some semblance of worth shines forth, and so hard do they try to reproduce the conduct of such men, that they even try to copy in their speech, dress and deportment certain of the faults of those whose virtue they admire. In fact, they apply themselves to aping the attire, behaviour and speech of kings, not simply from a desire to imitate them, but also in order to worm their way by flattery into the affections of the more powerful and by these arts to pursue wealth, office and authority. For they know that we are so constituted by nature as not only to love ourselves and our own concerns but also to cherish in others our own likeness, corrupt though it may be. Our attempts to obtain what we want by entreaty rather than by making arrogant and presumptuous demands are much more effective than legal threats, the display of penalties, or armed force. This is what brings the people back to obedience without violence, wins for the king the goodwill of his subjects, and increases and protects public peace and the wealth of private individuals. Let the king constantly bear in mind, therefore, that he stands on the world's stage, set there for all to look upon, and that nothing he says or does can be hidden: 'the vices of kings can never remain secret, for destiny's exalted light allows nothing to be concealed. Rumour makes its way into every hiding-place and searches out the remotest retreats.'[109] So how careful princes must be on both fronts, for neither their vices nor their virtues can be hidden, yet they cannot be divulged without causing far-reaching change.

If anyone still doubts how much influence the life of a prince can have in improving public behaviour, let him picture those early days when Rome was still in its infancy. When that people, ignorant of the finer arts, a collection of shepherds and strangers, not to put it more harshly, themselves warlike by nature and ruled by the most warlike of kings, had set up something like an armed camp with the aim of disturbing the peace of neighbouring peoples and challenging them to battle, how great do you think was the hatred and fear they inspired in their neighbours?[110] Yet when that same people had appointed for themselves a pious and just king, they were suddenly so changed that their neighbours thought it almost impious to injure a people devoted to justice and the worship of the gods – those very neighbours, I say, whose fields they had previously ravaged, whose towns they had burnt, and whose children and kinsmen they had carried off into slavery. But if Numa Pompilius, a king brought in only a little before then from a hostile nation,[111] could achieve so much among such barbarous manners and in an uncultured age, what shall we expect – or rather what shall we not expect – of those princes who, born and bred in the hope of power, obtain it with the support of kinsmen, retainers and inherited wealth? What a passion for virtue it must kindle in them that they are not simply hoping for a single day's fame, as with actors when a play has been well acted, but realise that they have the prospect of the good will and admiration of their own age, the everlasting esteem of posterity, and honours which are all but divine.

If only I could put into words the picture I have in my mind of that honour. But to give you some rough outline of it, imagine that bronze serpent which Moses set up in the Arabian desert, the mere sight of which was enough to cure bites inflicted by other serpents;[112] imagine a great crowd, some of them gathering together to obtain this potent remedy after they have been bitten by serpents, others astonished at this unheard of miracle, and all extolling the immense, incredible kindness of God with praise of every sort when they see the pains of a fatal wound alleviated, not by medicines which involve torment for the patient, toil for his doctors, and constant anxiety for his friends, but instead his restoration to health in a single moment and not through the long passage of time. Now compare a king with that serpent, but make the comparison in this way: count a good king among the greatest blessings of God, for he alone, without any expense or toil on his part, relieves all the afflictions of the kingdom, calms its disorders and reduces even long-standing sores to a slight scar; he is a healer not only to those who behold him face to face but to those who are so far away that they have no hope of seeing him. The picture of him carried in men's minds is so powerful that it easily achieves what the prudence of jurists, the knowledge of philosophers, or the experience of so many centuries in forming the arts has never been able to achieve. What greater honour, dignity, grandeur or majesty can be spoken or imagined for any man than that by his speech and converse, appearance and renown, in fact by the silent picture of him carried in men's minds, he restores those wallowing in luxury to moderation, the violent to equanimity and the mad to sanity? Can you, if you wish, ask God, ever kindly disposed to mankind, for any greater boon than this?

This is, if I am not mistaken, the true picture of a king, not that picture of him with his armed retinue around him, always afraid or making others afraid, measuring the people's hatred of him by his hatred of them.[113] This picture which we have given is painted in the most beautiful colours by Seneca in his *Thyestes*.[114] That work is so fine that I have no doubt that you must know it. Do you really think

now that my view of the king is disparaging and contemptuous, and
that I am, as you put it a little while ago, loading him with fetters and
locking him in a prison guarded by the laws? Or am I not rather
bringing him into the light, into the company of men and the public
theatre of the human race, not attended by an arrogant escort of
bodyguards and swordsmen and by silk-clad scoundrels, but safe in
his own innocence, protected not by the terror of arms but by the
love of the people, not only independent and exalted but honoured
and revered, sacred and majestic, proceeding amid auspicious omens
and cries of joyful approbation, and attracting the gaze and attention
of everyone wherever he goes? What ovation or triumph can be
compared with this daily procession? Or if God were to come down
to earth in human shape, what greater honour could men pay to Him
than that which would be shown to the true king, that is, the living
image of God?[115] No greater honour than this could be bestowed by
love or extorted by fear or devised by flattery. What do you think of
this picture of the king?

M. A brilliant picture, to be sure, and so splendid that nothing it
seems could be spoken or imagined in more splendid terms. But it is
difficult for such nobility of mind to be found amid the moral
corruption of our times, unless a careful education is combined with
an upright character and natural goodness. When a mind shaped
from youth by excellent precepts and principles, and matured by
age and experience, strives towards true glory by the path of virtue,
the blandishments of pleasure which tempt it and the assaults of
adversity which try to undermine it are of no avail. For so well does
'education bring out the innate force and proper training strengthen
the mind'[116] that it finds opportunity to practise virtue even amid
the enticements of pleasure, and virtue thinks it has been offered an
occasion for renown when it faces difficulties which usually terrify
weaker spirits. So since a liberal education is so important to every
aspect of life, what care and concern should be taken to ensure that
the tender young minds of kings are properly instructed right from

the very beginning. Good kings confer many benefits on their subjects, and conversely many disasters originate from bad princes. Hence the behaviour and inclinations of kings themselves and of others who administer supreme power along with them seem to me to have the greatest influence in every respect. What is done well or otherwise by private individuals is for the most part hidden from the multitude, or because of the man's obscurity his example affects only a few; but all the words and actions of those who manage the government of the commonwealth are written, as it were, on a votive tablet, to use Horace's phrase.[117] They cannot be hidden but are set before everyone for them to copy. They win over men's minds not merely through the desire to please but through the seductive attractions of self-interest, and public behaviour alters with shifts in the moods of kings. But my fear is that our kings will not allow themselves to be persuaded to fulfil the tasks which you specified a little while ago. They are so weakened by the allurements of pleasure and deluded by the deceitful semblance of honour that I think they do almost what some of the poets say happened to the Trojans who sailed with Paris.[118] After the real Helen had been left in Egypt with Proteus, a holy and god-like man, they struggled for ten years over her likeness with such stubbornness that the end of that most destructive of wars marked also the end of the wealthiest kingdom of those times. Once they have gained it by hook or by crook, headstrong tyrants cling to that false semblance of kingship, and can neither retain it without resorting to crime nor give it up without their own destruction. Yet if anyone were to tell them that the real Helen over whom they think they are fighting is hidden away somewhere else, they would regard him as mad.

B. I am of course glad that, although you have not really seen that daughter of Jupiter, this likeness of her, such as it is, gives you a partial understanding of her beauty. But if those who have to their own great cost been lovers of that false Helen were to see a perfect likeness of the true one painted to the life by some Protogenes or

Apelles,[119] I have no doubt they would admire her and love her to distraction, and, unless they at once told that other Helen to be about her business, they would suffer those severe penalties which Persius in his *Satires* calls down upon tyrants: 'Supreme father of the gods, when dread lust dipped in fiery poison has moved the minds of cruel tyrants, may it be your will to inflict only this punishment on them, that they should see virtue and pine away for having abandoned it.'[120] And in fact since we have happened to mention tyrants, would you like us to go straight on to deal with them?

M. Unless you think that some other subject should be dealt with first.

*

B. We shall be least likely to go wrong, I think, if in order to find the tyrant we proceed by the same path we used when we began our search for the king.[121]

M. I agree, for in that way we shall most easily understand the difference between them if they are arranged face to face for examination.

B. First of all, to begin with the name 'tyrant', I think it is uncertain what language it belongs to, so I believe it is superfluous to look for a Greek or Latin origin for it.[122] No one in fact who has applied himself to liberal studies with any diligence can, I think, be in any doubt over what the ancients called tyranny. The name tyrant was given both by the Greeks and the Romans to those who had unlimited power in all matters, bound by no legal restrictions and subject to no judicial investigation. So in both languages, as you know, not only heroes and outstanding men but also the greatest of the gods and even Jupiter himself are called tyrants, even by those who think and speak about the gods with reverence.[123]

M. I am well aware of that, and so I am all the more puzzled how it is that that name has for many centuries been accounted odious and even as one of the gravest insults.

B. Yes, this word seems to have had the same fate as a great many others. If you consider words in themselves, they are blameless, and although to the listeners' ears some sound smoother and others harsher, they have no power in themselves to excite men's minds to anger, hatred or joy, or in some other way to produce pleasure or annoyance. If anything like this happens to us, it usually arises not from the word but from the way men use it and from the image conceived by those who hear it. So a word which is respectable to some listeners cannot be heard by others without first apologising.

M. I remember something like this occurred with the names Nero and Judas. In one case for the Romans and in the other for the Jews, the name was considered the most distinguished and honourable in men of the highest rank. Subsequently, however, it has come about, not through the fault of the names themselves but through that of two men, that not even the most wicked wish to give these names to their children, such is the infamy into which they have sunk.[124]

B. Clearly the same thing also happened with the word tyrant. It is credible that the first magistrates to be so-called were good men, if only from the fact that the name was at one time held in such honour that it was even applied to the gods. It was their successors who made it so shameful by their crimes that everyone shunned it as if it were contagious and pestilential, deeming it a milder insult to be called a hangman than a tyrant.[125]

M. Perhaps the same thing happened in this case as with kings at Rome after the expulsion of the Tarquins and with the name dictator after the consulship of M. Antonius and P. Dolabella.[126]

B. Quite right. On the other hand, humble plebeian names have become renowned through the virtue of the men who chanced to bear them, such as Camillus, Metellus and Scrofa among the Romans,[127] and Henry, Genseric and Charles among the Germans.[128] You will understand this all the better if you consider that, while the name of tyrant became extinct, the institution itself endured and this type of authority retained its original honour among many illustrious nations, such as the *aesymnetae* among the Greeks, and the *dictatores* among the Romans. These were in each case legitimate tyrants: tyrants because they were more powerful than the laws, but legitimate because they were chosen with the consent of the people.[129]

M. What's this I hear? That there can actually be legitimate tyrants? I was certainly expecting something very different from you, but now you seem to be blurring the distinctions between all kings and tyrants.

B. As a matter of fact it seems that among the ancients kings and tyrants were exactly the same, but they lived, I think, in different periods. The name tyrant was the older, I presume; then when that became abhorrent their place was taken by kings, whose name was more attractive and whose authority was milder. As kings too degenerated, the moderating influence of laws was applied to set limits to their boundless desire for authority. As men sought after new remedies to fit the nature of the times and human behaviour, they found the old types of government abhorrent and looked for new ones. The discussion which we are pursuing at present concerns the two types of princely power: the type in which the authority of the laws is stronger than that of the kings, and the worst type of tyranny, in which everything is the opposite of kingship, and we have undertaken a comparison of these types.

M. Yes, and I am waiting eagerly for you to reach that topic.

B. We agreed at the beginning, then, that the king was appointed in order to preserve human society. We decided that his function was, as is laid down in the law, to give every man his due.[130]

M. I remember that.

B. First, then, what name shall we give to anyone who does not receive that office by the will of the people but seizes it by force or usurps it by fraud?

M. A tyrant, I suppose.

B. There are many other distinctions besides, but I shall run through them only briefly, as anyone can find them easily enough in Aristotle.[131] Kingly authority is in accordance with nature, that of a tyrant is contrary to it. A king rules over willing subjects, a tyrant over unwilling. Kingship is the princely power of a free man among free men, tyranny is that of a master over slaves. A king's subjects stand guard over him to ensure his safety, while strangers guard a tyrant in order to crush his subjects, for the one wields power on behalf of his subjects, the other for himself.

M. What about those who have gained supreme power by violence and without the consent of the people but have ruled their kingdoms for many years in such a way that the people have not regretted their government? Apart from the fact that they were not lawfully elected, how very little was lacking in Hiero of Syracuse in the past or in Cosimo di Medici of Florence today if you consider the function of a legitimate king?[132]

B. We cannot remove them from the category of tyrants. It was very well put by a distinguished historian that 'to use force to rule your country or your subjects, even though you may have the power and may amend their faults, is nevertheless offensive'.[133] Again, it seems to me that such men act like robbers who, by making a suitable division of their ill-gotten gains, seek the praise of justice for their injustice and of liberality for their theft. But they do not achieve their aim. For the hatred aroused by a single misdeed loses them all gratitude for their ostentatious generosity; and so much the less do they inspire their subjects' confidence in their public-spiritedness when they behave in this way for the sake of their own absolute power rather than the advantage of their people. Clearly, their intention is to enjoy their own pleasures more safely and, once the people's hatred has been softened a little, to lay firm foundations for the rule of their descendants. When they have achieved this they revert to their true character. What harvest will follow can easily be appreciated from the sowing.[134] For to refer everything to the will of a single man and to transfer to him power over all the laws has the same effect as annulling them altogether. This type of tyrant might perhaps be tolerable if he could not be removed without public ruin, just as we endure certain diseases of the body rather than expose our lives to the hazardous risk of some dubious cure. But those who openly wield power not for their country but for themselves, who take account not of the public interest but of their own pleasure, who found the stability of their authority on the weakness of their subjects, and who see their kingship not as a commission entrusted to them by God but as plunder for the taking; such men are not joined to us by any bond of civility or common humanity but must be adjudged the most deadly enemies of God and man. All the measures taken by kings must have regard not for their own wealth in particular but for the well-being of their subjects in general. The more kings are raised above the rank of other men, the more they must imitate the heavenly bodies which, won over by none of our observances, nevertheless pour on human affairs the life-giving and beneficent force of their heat and light. Even the very titles which we have used to pay honour to kings, if you recall them, should bring this munificence to mind.

M. I think I recall them: you mean that they were to show a father's kindness towards their subjects, who were entrusted to them like children, and a shepherd's care in looking after their interests, in saving them from harm [*the skill of a helmsman; likewise, in showing fairness,*] they should behave like generals, like leaders in the excellence of their virtues, and like commanders in bidding them do what will be to their advantage.

B. Then can we call someone a father if he treats subjects like slaves, or a shepherd if he flays his flock rather than feeds it,[135] or a helmsman if he is always anxious to throw the cargo overboard, or if, as the saying goes, he scuttles the ship in which he himself is sailing?[136]

M. Certainly not.

B. What about the ruler whose commands are not in the interest of the people but who is concerned for himself alone? Who does not vie with the good in virtue but strives by his vices to outdo whoever is most vicious? Who leads his own people into manifest snares?

M. Assuredly, I shall not regard him as a general, a commander or a leader.

B. If you see anyone, therefore, who usurps the name of king yet does not surpass any of the mass of the people in any kind of virtue but is even inferior to many, who does not bestow a father's love on his subjects but crushes them under his arrogant dominion, who thinks that his flock is entrusted to him not for safekeeping but for gain, will you think that this man is truly a king, even if he goes about with a numerous train of attendants, flaunts himself in magnificent finery, inflicts summary punishments, wins over the mob and courts their applause by means of prizes, games and processions, even by outrageous buildings,[137] and whatever else passes for magnificence? Will you regard this man as a king, I ask you?

M. No, not if I wish to be consistent. I would see him instead as a man with no place in human society.

B. What are the limits within which you confine this human society?

M. Those same limits by which you seemed in your earlier remarks to want it to be restricted: I mean the barriers of the law, for I see that bandits, thieves and adulterers who overstep these are publicly punished, and that it is held to be a just ground for punishment that they have gone beyond the bounds of human society.

B. What about those who have never wanted to come within those bounds?

M. I think they must be regarded as the enemies of God and of men, and must be classed as wolves or some other type of dangerous beast rather than as human beings.[138] If anyone rears such beasts, he is rearing destruction for himself and for others; whoever kills them benefits not only himself but the whole community. If I were allowed to pass a law, I would order, as the Romans used to do in seeking expiation for monsters, that men like that should be banished into desert lands or drowned in the sea far from the sight of land, lest even the contagion of their dead bodies infect living men;[139] and that those who killed them would have rewards decreed to them, not only by the people as a whole but by individuals, as commonly happens in the case of those who have killed wolves or bears or have caught their cubs.[140] If any monster of this kind were born, even if it spoke with a human voice and had the face of a man and resembled him in every other part, I would not believe that I had anything in common with him. Or if someone were to strip off his human shape and sink to such barbarity, refusing to mix with other men except to destroy them, I think that he is no more fit to be called a man than are monkeys, apes or bears, even though by his looks, gestures and speech he simulated a man.

B. Now, if I am not mistaken, you understand what the wisest of the ancients held to be the nature of a king and likewise of a tyrant. Do you want me, then, as I did in delineating a king, to put before you some such model of a tyrant?

M. Yes, I should like that very much indeed, if it is not too much trouble.

B. You have not forgotten, I suppose, what is said by the poets about the Furies and by our own writers about the nature of evil spirits: namely, that there are spirits hostile to the human race who, since they themselves are suffering eternal tortures, delight in the torments of men.[141] This, I assure you, is the true picture of tyranny. But because this picture can be discerned only in the mind and not with the aid of the senses, I shall put before you another picture which can rouse the senses as well as the mind, and, as it were, come right before your eyes. Imagine that you see a ship tempest-tossed at sea, with all the shores around it not only harbourless but full of the most deadly of enemies; now imagine the master of that ship struggling with his passengers in mutual hatred, having no other hope of safety than the loyalty of his crew – an uncertain hope, since he is well aware that he is entrusting his life to men of the most barbarous kind, devoid of all human feeling, whose favour he retains only by money and who can be turned against him by the prospect of greater gain.[142] Such is the life, I assure you, which tyrants embrace as a blessed one. They fear their enemies abroad and their subjects at home, and not just their subjects but their servants, kinsmen, brothers, wives, children and parents. [*And the more upright each one of these people is, the more terrible he is to the tyrants.*] So at all times they are either waging or dreading foreign war with their neighbours, civil war with their subjects, or family feuds with their own households. They can expect no help but from mercenaries, yet dare neither hire the good nor trust the bad. What, I ask you, can bring them any pleasure in life?

Dionysius, for fear of letting a razor near his throat, took away from his grown-up maiden daughters the task of shaving his beard.[143] Timoleon slew his brother,[144] Alexander of Pherae was murdered by his wife,[145] Spurius Cassius by his father.[146] What torment do you think he, who has these examples always before his eyes, carries around in his heart when he reflects that he has set himself up as a target for all mankind to shoot at, and when he is not only racked in his waking hours by the torments of his conscience but roused from his sleep by terrifying visions of the living and the dead and pursued by the Furies with their torches? The time which nature has given to all living creatures for rest, and to men as a relief also from their cares, is for the tyrant turned into horror and torture.

*

M. These explanations of yours are certainly clever enough, and, for all I know, they may be sound. But if I am not mistaken they do not contribute much to our purpose.[147] For those who have the power to choose the kings they wish also have the power to constrain those they elect by whatever laws they please. But you know that in our country kings are not elected but are born, and I have always thought that, no less than the kingdom itself, their inheritance was that their will should have the force of law. I did not come to this conclusion lightly, but on the basis of weighty authorities, in whose company I am not ashamed to err – if indeed I am in error. For not to mention any others, the jurists maintain that by the 'royal law' which defined their authority, all the power of the people was transferred to the kings so that what is pleasing to them must be regarded as the law.[148] No doubt it was this law which gave rise to those threats of a certain emperor that with a single edict he would take from the jurists all the knowledge of which they boasted so much.[149]

B. You acted wisely when, in citing the worst authority for such a serious matter, you thought that his name should be suppressed. For it was C. Caligula, who even desired that the whole Roman people should have a single neck.[150] In that emperor there was nothing human, far less regal, except his outward shape. So you must be aware how much weight his authority deserves to have. But as far as the 'royal law' is concerned, the legal experts themselves do not explain its nature, or when, by whom and in what terms it was enacted. The Roman kings never had that power, since there was a right of appeal from them to the people.[151] No one ever regarded as a law that bill by which L. Flaccus established the tyranny of L. Sulla when the freedom of the Roman people had been crushed through the silencing of other laws. The effect of that proposal was that whatever L. Sulla did was to be considered valid.[152] No free people has ever been so senseless as to grant this right over itself willingly; or if such a people existed, they were certainly worthy of being forever enslaved to tyrants and of paying the penalty for their folly. But if there was a law of this nature, let us believe it was an example set before us as a warning and not as a model.

M. Unquestionably you are right to give this warning, but your admonition applies to those who have it in their power to appoint over themselves kings of whatever kind. It has nothing at all to do with us, who do not choose the best by our votes, but accept those offered by chance. The point made by the jurist does seem properly to concern us, for we granted the ancestors of our kings precisely that right over us and our posterity that they and their posterity should hold authority over us in perpetuity. I only wish you could have given your warning to them (I mean our ancestors) who were free to take as their kings whomever they pleased. Now, however, the value of that belated advice of yours is not that we can correct what is no longer in our power but that we can deplore the folly of our ancestors and acknowledge the wretchedness of our position. What is left for us to do, handed over into slavery as we were, except to pay the penalty for the folly of others, alleviating it by patient endurance and refraining from any untimely commotion which might provoke the anger of those whose authority we cannot reject, whose power we cannot diminish, and whose might and violence we cannot escape? But that 'royal law' to which you are so greatly opposed was not devised to gratify tyrants, as you wish it to appear, since it was approved by that most just of emperors, Justinian, in whose eyes such open flattery would have found no favour.[153] For in the case of a foolish prince those words are true: 'Who delights in baseless honour and is terrified by false notoriety except the man who is faulty and false?'[154]

B. Admittedly Justinian was a great man, as histories tell us, although some say that he was cruelly ungrateful to Belisarius.[155] But even if he was the kind of man you believe him to have been, you may nevertheless recall that those who were more or less his contemporaries recount that Tribonian, outstanding among those who introduced those laws, was by far the most wicked of men and one who could easily have been persuaded to gratify even the worst of princes.[156] Even good princes do not shun this kind of flattery; for 'even those who do not wish to kill anyone want to have the power to do so', and 'there is nothing which power equal to the gods dare not believe about itself when it is praised'.[157] But let us return to our own princes, to whom you say the kingdom comes by inheritance, not by election. I speak only of our own, for if I were to digress to foreign princes I am afraid that our discourse would be longer than we had planned.

M. Yes, I think you should return to our own kings. For foreign affairs are not very relevant to our present discussion.

B. Then, to begin at the very beginning, we are quite agreed that it was their reputation for virtue which made us choose princes to rule over the rest of us.

M. So our historians relate.[158]

B. Likewise it is agreed that many who used their office cruelly and scandalously were called to account by their subjects, that some were condemned to imprisonment for life, others punished in some cases with exile, in others with death. Even when their sons or kinsmen were chosen in their place, no judicial inquiry was ever decreed against their killers.[159] Nowhere on earth, however, was more severe punishment exacted from those who had harmed good kings. Since it would be tedious to go over these cases one by one, I shall mention a few of the most recent, of which we have a fresher recollection. The murder of James I, who left as his heir a six year old boy, was punished so severely by the nobles that they put to death men born of the most distinguished families, pre-eminent for their wealth and dependants, using a new and exquisite form of execution.[160] On the other hand, who mourned, let alone avenged, the death of James III, an infamous and cruel man?[161] In the case of the death of his son James IV, the mere suspicion of a crime was punished with death.[162] Our ancestors were not only respectful towards good kings, but they were also lenient and merciful towards those who were bad. For when Culen, on his way to answer the charges brought against him, was killed by one of his enemies, the murderer received the severest of penalties by order of the Estates.[163] Likewise Evenus, already condemned to life-long imprisonment, was killed in prison by an enemy, and his murderer suffered the same penalties. Although everyone loathed Evenus' abominable life, they avenged his violent death as if it had been a case of parricide.[164]

M. At present I am not so much asking what has occasionally happened in the past as by what right our kings reign over us.

B. To return to that topic, then, just as in the case of our early kings down to Kenneth III, who was the first to settle the kingdom in his own family, it is clear what power the people had in appointing kings and in holding them to account, so it must follow either that Kenneth made this change against the will of the people or that he gained their approval by persuasion.[165]

M. That cannot be denied.

B. Well then, if he compelled the people to obey him by force, it will be open to the people to throw off that enforced authority as soon as they begin to feel confidence in their own strength. For the laws received by kings and peoples declare, and nature herself cries out, that whatever is done by force can similarly be undone by force.[166]

M. What if the people, either deceived by fraud or compelled by fear, have given themselves into slavery? What reason can be put forward why they should not adhere forever to what has been once agreed?

B. If you are arguing with me on the basis of an agreement, why should I not from the opposite point of view suggest reasons why pacts and agreements should be dissolved? Firstly, there is in all commonwealths a fixed law, drawn from the springs of nature, concerning agreements which are entered into because of violence or fear.[167] The laws also grant full restitution to those outwitted by fraud, and this principle they think should apply particularly to minors and those persons whom they wish to enjoy the fullest rights.[168] What community of men, therefore, may more justly demand restitution than the people as a whole? When an injury is done to the people, it is not done merely to one single part of the commonwealth but reaches into every limb of the body politic.

M. I know that this law is invoked in the case of private individuals and that it is not unfair to anyone. But there is no need for us to discuss this at length, since it is far more likely (as is related by the historians also) that that right was granted to kings by the will of the people.[169]

B. It is credible too that a concession of such importance was not made without very good reason.

M. I readily agree.

B. What, then, do you think was the main reason?

M. What else but the reason given by the historians? Weariness with electioneering,[170] rebellions, murders, civil wars, involving often the destruction of one of the parties and always very great loss to both. For in order to pass a more peaceable kingdom on to their children, those who gained possession of it would try to annihilate their brothers and almost all their closest kin, just as we hear happens among the Turks and we see happening among clan chiefs in our islands and in Ireland.[171]

B. To which do you think that strife was more destructive, the people or the princes?

M. To the kings certainly, since the greater part of the people usually look on unconcerned at the rivalries of princes, and always fall as booty to the victors.

B. Then it was, it seems, for their own sakes rather than for the good of the people that princes wanted to establish the throne firmly in their own family.

M. Probably.

B. Now it is likely that, in order to gain something so vital to the lasting honour, wealth and security of their family, they gave up some of their rights in return; and that they made some concession on their part in order to retain more easily the good will and approval of the people and win their consent.

M. I believe so.

B. You will at least grant me that it is incredible that, in return for bestowing such a great privilege on their kings, the people should allow themselves to have less favourable rights than they had before.

M. Quite incredible.

B. And the kings would not have striven for it so eagerly if they had known it would be harmful and injurious both to their children and to the people.

M. By no means.

B. So imagine someone from the ranks of an assembly of a free people freely asking the king: 'What if some king has a stupid son? What if he is mad? Will you establish as our rulers those who cannot rule themselves?'[172]

M. I do not think there was any need to make this qualification, since this situation is provided for by the laws.[173]

B. Well said. So let us consider this point: if kings had been granted by the people power unhindered by the laws, surely that power would have been useless to them, especially to those who wanted to take account of the future prospects of their family?

M. But in what sense could we believe that that power would be useless?

B. Because nothing tends more to the permanence of government than that temperate exercise of authority which is both honourable for kings and equitable and beneficial to the people. The human mind possesses something lofty and noble implanted in it by nature which makes it obedient to no one unless what he commands is beneficial; and nothing is more effective in holding human society together than the exchange of benefits.[174] Theopompus, therefore, seems to have responded wisely when his wife rebuked him because he had diminished the strength of his authority by the addition of the ephors and would leave for his sons less royal power than he had inherited: 'So much the stronger', he said.[175]

M. What you say about permanence is, I think, perfectly true. The kingdoms of the Scots and the Danes are, I believe, by far the most ancient of all those in Europe, and they seem to me to have achieved this by no other means than the moderate exercise of supreme power, whereas meanwhile the kingdoms of the French, the English and the Spanish have passed so many times from one family to another.[176] Yet I am not sure that those kings of ours were as wise as Theopompus.

B. Even if they did not show so much foresight, do you think the people were so foolish that they let slip such a convenient opportunity when it was offered, or so smitten with fear or seduced by flattery that they gave themselves up voluntarily to slavery?

M. Perhaps not. But suppose, as is possible, that they were too blind to see what was to their own advantage, or that, although they did see it, they were so careless of their own interests that they scorned it. Will they not be deservedly punished for their folly?

B. It is unlikely that anything of the kind took place, since we see that right up to our own times the contrary practice has been observed. Apart from the fact that whenever evil kings have set out to tyrannise over their subjects they have always been punished, some traces of the old custom still survive in ancient families. For the original Scots, right up to our own times, elect their chiefs, and once elected associate with him a council of elders; those chiefs who do not obey this council are deprived of their office.[177] If this practice is still observed with the utmost care in certain parts of the kingdom, would they ignore it when the welfare of the whole was at stake? And would they willingly surrender themselves into bondage under one who instead of a privilege was to possess a legitimate kingship?[178] Having won their freedom by their valour, defended it by arms, and retained it without interruption through so many centuries, would they give it away without violence and without war to someone who did not expect to receive it? Apart from the penalties so often exacted from them for misgovernment of the kingdom, the disaster suffered by John Balliol shows that our kings never possessed the power you speak of. Balliol was deposed by the nobility some 260 years ago because he had subjected himself and his kingdom to the authority of Edward of England, and Robert I was installed in his place.[179] The same example also demonstrates that that custom continued unbroken right from the earliest times.

M. What custom do you mean?

B. When our kings are publicly inaugurated, they give a solemn promise to the entire people that they will observe the laws, customs and ancient practices of our ancestors, and that they will adhere to that law which they have received from them.[180] This is shown by the entire order of ceremonies and by the first visits which the kings pay to individual towns.[181] All this makes it easy to see the nature of the power which they received from our ancestors, namely, the same as is held by those who, having been chosen by election, swear to observe the laws. God set down this condition under which David and his descendants should reign: He promises that they will reign as long as they obey those laws ordained by Him.[182] These facts make it probable that the power received by our kings from our ancestors was not unbounded but was limited and restricted within fixed boundaries. There was, too, the confirmation given by the passage of time and the exercise of this right by the people without interruption, an exercise never censured in any public decree.

M. But I am afraid that it may not be easy to ensure that kings are swayed by that probability you mention and submit to these laws, even if the laws have been accepted under oath or have been applied by the people.

B. I for my part believe that it is no less difficult to persuade the people to forego a right received from their ancestors, sanctioned by the usage of so many centuries and uniformly exercised without interruption. Nor do I think it necessary to guess what they are likely to do when I can see what they have done. If through the resolute determination of both parties recourse is had to war, the victor will indeed impose whatever law he pleases on the vanquished; but he will be able to do so only until the defeated party regains its strength and takes up arms again. Such struggles are usually fought to a finish, always with destruction to the people, but generally with the ruin of the kings as well. For it is from this one source that the extinction of every kingdom derives.

M. It must happen like that.

B. I have perhaps traced this further back than was necessary, so that you might understand clearly the nature of the old law of kingship in our nation. If I had been dealing with you more exactingly, I could have used a much shorter route to reach the point I wanted.

M. Although you have almost convinced me already, I shall gladly listen to you explain the nature of that route.

B. Then I would like you first to answer this question: do you approve of the definition of a law which is put forward by jurists who say that a law is what the people have enacted following a proposal made by someone with the right to propose it?[183]

M. Yes, I approve of it.

B. And we agreed that when faults are detected in the laws, they can either be amended or repealed by those same people who enacted them.

M. We did.

B. And you see, I think, that those who are our kings by birth are appointed by the laws and by the votes of the people no less than those we said were elected from the start; and that, as the makers of the laws, the people will not lack for remedies, not only against violence and fraud, but also against neglect in submitting to the laws.

M. Certainly, I see that.

B. The only difference is that the law relating to our kings was passed several centuries ago. At the beginning of a new reign it is usual to give approval to an old law, not to pass a new one. In countries which hold assemblies to elect each particular king, it is customary to enact the law, make and approve the king, and begin the new reign at the same time.

M. That is so.

B. Let us now, if you will, summarise briefly from the beginning what we have agreed, so that there is an opportunity to change our minds if anything has been approved without due consideration.

M. Agreed.

B. First of all we decided that the king is chosen for the sake of his people, and that heaven can grant us nothing finer than a good king and nothing more pernicious than a bad one.

M. Correct.

B. We said also that a bad king is called a tyrant.

M. Yes, we did.

B. And because there is not such a profusion of good men that there are always men of integrity for us to choose, nor such good fortune that the accident of birth always provides good men, we take as our kings, not men such as we might desire, but such as either the general will has approved or chance has offered. Moreover, that risk which exists either in electing new kings or in approving those offered by accident of birth was the reason why we desired laws which would set limits to their authority. And these laws should be nothing other than the manifest image (in so far as we can attain it) of a good prince.

M. That too we acknowledged.

B. It now remains for us, I think, to consider the punishment of tyrants.

M. That seems to be the one remaining point.[184]

*

B. What do you think should be done, then, if the king bursts through all the fetters of the laws and clearly behaves like a public enemy?

M. I am really at a loss. For although the arguments you have expounded seem to prove that we should have no association with such a king, yet so great is the strength of age-old custom that for me it has the force of law.[185] It is fixed so stubbornly in men's minds that, if it leads to a mistake from time to time, it is better to put up with it than to weaken the condition of the whole body in our efforts to cure a disease made less painful by long familiarity. For such is the nature of some diseases that it is better to endure the suffering they bring than to search for uncertain remedies. When these are tried, even if they are otherwise successful, they nevertheless bring such acute pain during treatment that the cure is more dangerous than the disease itself. Next, a point which concerns me more, I see that what you call tyranny is sanctioned by the Word of God, and what you denounce as the destruction of the laws, God calls the law of kingship. The authority of that passage influences me more than all the arguments of the philosophers.[186] Unless you extricate me from this difficulty, the fictions devised by men will not have enough weight to prevent me from defecting immediately to the enemy.

B. I see that you share the general error, and a most serious one it is, of trying to support one tyranny with another. How great is the tyranny of habit once it has become deeply rooted in men's minds, we have seen for ourselves all too often in this century, and that ancient historian Herodotus reminds us by an old illustration.[187] But I have no need to use old examples; consult your own experience instead. Consider how many occasions there are, and these far from insignificant, on which in accordance with reason you have abandoned the inveterate customs of so many centuries, and have thus been able to learn from your personal experiences that no path is more strewn with dangers than that public highway which they bid us to follow. Look closely at that road, I beg you; how much destruction, how much carnage you will see on it! But if this point is, as they say, clear as day, there is no reason for me to linger any more over proving or illustrating a matter which is self-evident. But as for that passage from the history of the kings which you allude to rather than explain, take care, I beg you, not to assume that the Lord has granted to kings what He detests in the life of tyrants.[188] To avoid making this mistake, I urge you to consider, first, what the people asked of the Lord; next, what motives they had for this novel request; and finally, what answer the Lord gave to the people. Firstly they ask for a king. But what kind of king? A lawful king? But they already had one. For Samuel had been given to them by the Lord, in Whose hands lay the right to appoint a ruler. For many years Samuel had administered justice to them in due accordance with the provisions of the laws of God. But when his sons administered justice during his old age, they did many things wickedly and gave judgements contrary to the laws. So far I see no reason why they should beg, or at least desire, of God a revolution in the form of government rather than an amendment to it, seeing that He had not long before destroyed the whole family of Eli root and branch for a very similar reason.[189] What, then, do they ask for? A king such as the neighbouring peoples had, who would be a judge at home and a commander in the field. But these kings were really tyrants, for as the peoples of Asia are more servile in spirit than Europeans, so they submitted more readily to the authority of tyrants, and to the best of my knowledge no mention is ever made by historians of a lawful king in Asia.[190] Besides, it is readily apparent that it is a tyrant, not a king, who is described here, if only from the fact that in Deuteronomy God had already prescribed a covenant for them which was not only different from this but even quite contrary to it. Samuel and the other judges had passed judgement for so many years in accordance with this covenant; when they rejected it, the Lord complains that He has been rejected by them.[191]

M. But everywhere the Lord uses the term king, not tyrant.

B. He does indeed call him a king, for it is characteristic of the Lord to use the language of the people whenever He addresses them. So He uses a word which is shared with ordinary people, but in case the ambiguous use of this word might deceive anyone He explains clearly how it was used among neighbouring peoples.

M. Even if what you say is true, there is more weight for us in those words of Paul, who tells us to pray for the well-being of princes, so far is he from allowing us to reject their authority, much less to remove them from the throne, and to slaughter them once they have been removed. Moreover, what princes does he commend to our prayers? The most cruel who ever existed, such as Tiberius, Caligula, Claudius and Nero, for the epistles of Paul are more or less contemporary with them.[192]

B. I think you are right in holding that Paul's authority is so great that a single sentence of his has more weight for you than the writings of all the philosophers and jurists. But be careful that you have weighed his opinions properly; for it is necessary to consider not only his words, but also when he wrote them, to whom, and why. First, then, let us see what Paul wrote. He writes to Titus (chapter 3): 'Remind them to be submissive to princes and powers, to obey at a word and to be ready for every good work.'[193] You see, I imagine, how he here defines the limits of obedience. He likewise writes to Timothy (chapter 2) that we should pray for all men, even for kings and for other magistrates, 'in order that,' as he puts it, 'we may live a peaceable life, in all godliness and honesty.'[194] You see here too what he lays down as the purpose of prayer, namely, not the well-being of kings, but the tranquillity of the church. From this it will not be difficult to grasp also the form of the prayer. And in his Epistle to the Romans he defines a king with almost dialectical precision: he says that the king is an officer to whom the sword has been given by God to punish the evil and to encourage and sustain the good.[195] 'These things are not written by Paul of a tyrant,' says Chrysostom, 'but of a true and lawful magistrate, who is the earthly representative of the true God; whoever resists him certainly resists the ordinance of God.'[196] Although we should pray for evil princes, however, we need not immediately conclude from this that their faults are to go unpunished, any more than those of robbers, for whom we are also told to pray; and if a good prince must be obeyed, it does not follow that a bad one must not be resisted. But if you also consider what induced Paul to write these words, note that this passage may count strongly against you. For Paul wrote it in order to censure the rashness of certain men who denied that the commands of magistrates were necessary for Christians. Since the power of magistrates was ordained to deal with evil men so that we might all live by impartial laws and an example of divine justice might be constantly in the midst of men, they claimed that it was of no relevance to those who were so far removed from the contagion of vice as to be a law unto themselves.[197] Paul, then, is not concerned here with those who act as magistrates but with magistracy itself, that is, with the function and duty of those who are set over others; and he is not concerned with any particular type of magistracy, but with the form of every lawful magistracy. His argument is not with those who think that bad magistrates ought to be restrained, but with those who reject the authority of all magistrates. On the basis of an absurd interpretation of Christian liberty, these men declared that it was shameful that those who had been set free by the Son of God and were ruled by the Spirit of God should submit to the power of any man. In order to refute their error Paul showed that magistracy is not only good but also sacred, the ordinance of God, indeed, expressly established to hold groups and communities of men together in such a way that they would recognise the blessings of God towards them and refrain from injuring one another. God commanded that those who were appointed to hold office should be the guardians of His laws.[198]

Now if we admit that the laws are good, as indeed they are, we must also admit that their guardians are worthy of honour and that the office filled by the guardians is something good and useful. Yet a magistrate inspires fear. But in whom? In the good or the bad? He is not a terror to the good, since he protects them from harm; but if he is a terror to the bad, that does not affect you, who are ruled by the Spirit of God. What need is there, then, you will say, for me to be subject to a magistrate, if I am the freedman of God? No, to prove that you are the freedman of the Lord, obey His laws.[199] The Spirit of God, by which you claim to be ruled, is likewise the maker of the laws, the support of magistrates and the author of obedience to them. We shall easily agree in this respect as well, therefore, that even in the best commonwealth a magistrate is needed, and that he must be honoured in every possible way. If someone disagrees with this, we think him mad and detestable and deserving of every kind of punishment, for he openly opposes the will of God revealed to us in Scripture. As far as Caligula, Nero, Domitian and other tyrants of that kind are concerned, you will find nothing in Paul to show why they should not be punished for violating the laws of God and of man. For he discusses the power of magistrates as such, not how evil men evilly wield that power. Indeed, if you measure tyrants of that kind against Paul's rule, they will not be magistrates at all. If anyone maintains that even bad princes are ordained by God, beware of the sophistry of such talk. Applying a hard wedge to a hard knot, as the saying goes,[200] God sometimes appoints an evil man to punish evil men, but no one in his right mind will dare to assert that God is the author of human malice, just as everyone knows that He is responsible for punishing evildoers. A good magistrate, again, generally chooses an evil man as executioner in punishing the guilty. However, although the magistrate appoints the executioner to his office, he does not immediately grant him immunity for every crime, nor does he intend him to be so far above the laws as not to be answerable to them.

I shall not linger any more over this comparison, lest court sycophants cry out that I speak of the supreme magistrate with too little respect. But for all their protests, they certainly cannot deny that the executioner's function is part of the public, perhaps even the royal, office. Even the kings themselves testify to this, for every time one of their public officials is injured, they complain that their own majesty and person have been violated.[201] Now the punishment of the guilty falls, if anything does, within the scope of the king's office. What about governors of cities or camp commandants? Or praetors? Or the consuls themselves? Does Paul tell us to be obedient to them as well or [*does he recognise a single princely power? As to the other magistrates*] does he regard them as private individuals? It is customary for all magistrates, not just the lesser ones but also those who are equal to kings, to be called to account for misuse of their authority. So I should like those who fondly imagine that so much power has been granted to kings by Paul's words either to show from the same Paul that only kings are meant here by the term power, and that therefore they alone are to be exempt from the penalties imposed by the laws; or if, when we speak of powers, we mean other magistrates as well, ordained by the same author, God, for the same purpose, I should again like them to show where it is that all magistrates are declared to be above the laws and free from the fear of punishment, or where such immunity is granted to kings alone and denied to others who are set up in authority.[202]

M. But Paul wishes everyone to be subject to the higher powers.

B. Yes, that is his command; but under the term power he of necessity comprehends all other magistrates as well, unless perhaps we believe that Paul thinks that in commonwealths which are without royal authority there is no government but sheer anarchy.[203]

M. I do not believe that, nor is it likely; and I am the more firmly of this opinion because all the more learned commentators on this passage agree with your view. They too believe that that argument of Paul's was aimed at those who maintained that no laws and magistracies whatever were applicable to them.[204]

B. And what about the point I made a little while back? Do you believe that those tyrants, the cruellest of all, are covered by Paul's words?

M. Yes indeed, for what evidence can you offer why I should not believe it? Especially since Jeremiah so earnestly, and with divine inspiration, admonishes the Jews to obey the king of the Assyrians and not to reject his authority for any reason?[205] From this it is inferred, on the same principle, that one should obey other tyrants as well, however monstrous they are.

B. To reply first to your second point: it is important for you to note that the prophet does not command the Jews to obey all tyrants but only the king of the Assyrians. If you wish to infer a legal principle from what is ordained in one particular case, first, you know very well – for dialectic has taught you – how absurdly you would be proceeding; and next, you will be in danger of being attacked with the same weapons by the opponents of tyranny. For either you must show what is so special about this case which makes you put it forward as a model to be copied by everyone everywhere; or, if you cannot do that, it must be admitted that, in the case of other particular instructions of God, whatever is ordained concerning any single individual must apply equally to all. If you once admit this, as you must, you will immediately have to face the objection that Ahab was also killed at God's command and that a reward was promised and duly given to his killer, also by divine command.[206] So when you take refuge in the argument that all tyrants must be obeyed because God through His prophet ordered His people to obey one particular tyrant, you will receive the immediate response that all tyrants must be killed by their subjects since it was at God's bidding that Ahab was killed by the commander of his own troops. I advise you, therefore, to find some more solid defence for tyrants in Scripture, or to leave Scripture aside for the present and return to the teaching of the philosophers.

M. I shall have to think about that. Meanwhile, however, let us return to the point where we digressed. Tell me, what passage can you cite in the Scriptures which allows that tyrants may be killed with impunity?

B. First of all, I submit that there is a clear injunction to do away with crime and criminals without any exception of rank or degree, but nowhere in the Holy Scriptures is greater protection given to tyrants than to private individuals. Next, that the definition of a power laid down by Paul does not apply to tyrants at all, since they devote the strength of their authority to the fulfilment of their own desires, not to the benefit of the people. Furthermore, one should note carefully how highly Paul valued bishops, whose function he praises warmly and sincerely, as they are in a certain way equivalent to kings and form their counterparts so far as the nature of their respective activities permits.[207] For bishops are physicians for internal diseases, and kings for external ones, but Paul did not want either of them to be exempt and free from the authority of the other. But just as bishops are subject to kings in the conduct of their lives in temporal affairs, so too kings must obey the spiritual admonitions given by bishops.[208] However, I assure you that, great though the prestige and standing of these bishops may be, no law, divine or human, exempts them from punishment for their crimes. To say nothing of the others, the pope himself, who is held to be, as it were, the bishop of bishops, and who rises so far above the highest rank of every king that he wishes to be treated as a kind of god among men, is not exempted from the penalties of the laws even by his own canon lawyers, a class of men devoted above all others to him.[209] Since they deemed it absurd that God – they do not hesitate to give him this name – should be liable to the censure of men, and yet believed that it was unjust that the greatest crimes and foulest acts should go unpunished in anyone, they devised a principle by which crimes would be punished and yet the pope would remain sacrosanct and inviolable. For they judged the rights of the Pope to be one thing and those of the man who is Pope to be another, and while they exempt the Pope, who (they maintain) cannot err, from trial by law, they admit nevertheless that the man who is Pope is liable to faults and to punishment for his faults. And they have made their view clear no less in the severity of their condemnation than in the subtlety of their argument.[210]

It would be tedious to show which pontiffs, or, to use their way of putting it, which of those who have taken the role of pontiff, have not only been compelled while still living to abdicate their office but even dragged from their tombs when dead and thrown into the Tiber.[211] But to omit older illustrations, the memory of Paul IV still remains fresh in men's minds. His own city of Rome recently testified to the general hatred of him by a novel kind of decree. For the anger from which he had been saved was vented on his kinsmen, his statues and his portraits.[212] This interpretation by which we separate the power from the person who wields it ought not to seem too subtle to you, since it is a distinction recognised by philosophy, approved by commentators of old, and not unknown to the uneducated mob, strangers though they are to subtle disputation. Working men do not take it as a slur on their trade if some smith or baker is punished for robbery, but rather they rejoice that their guild has been purged of criminals. If anyone feels otherwise, I think he should be afraid of appearing to deplore, not the disgrace incurred by his guild, but rather the punishment of the men with whom he is associated by complicity in their wicked crimes. In my view, if kings dispensed with the advice of criminals and sycophants, and measured their greatness by the respect paid to their virtues rather than by their impunity for misdeeds, they would not be offended at the punishment of tyrants nor think their royal majesty infringed by their destruction, however it comes about. No, they would instead be glad that it had been purged of such a vile and shameful stain, especially since they are usually extremely angry, and with every justification, at robbers who use the king's name to cloak their misdeeds.

M. And rightly so. But I would like you to leave these matters aside and proceed to the other headings you mentioned.

B. What headings do you mean, tell me?

M. I mean the question of when and to whom Paul wrote these things. I am eager to know what this has to do with the present argument.

B. Here too your wish shall be gratified. First of all, to deal with the times, Paul wrote this in the very infancy of the church, when it was necessary not only to be above reproach, but also to avoid giving any opportunity for criticism to those looking even for unjust grounds for making accusations. Next, he wrote to men brought together into a single community from different races and indeed from the whole body of the Roman Empire. Among them there were few who were notable for their wealth; hardly anyone who held or had held a magistracy; not so very many who had the status of citizens, and these mainly of foreign birth or even to a large extent of freedman rank; while the rest were mostly artisans and slaves.[213] Among them were some who extended Christian liberty further than the plain sense of the Gospel permitted. This multitude, then, drawn from the motley crowd of ordinary folk, earning a meagre living by heavy labour, were inevitably less concerned with the form of government, the extent of the empire, or the life and duties of kings, than with public tranquillity and domestic peace. Nor by law could they claim anything more for themselves than to live quietly under the protection of whatever authority there was. If such people had tried to take any part in government, they would inevitably have been thought not only foolish but quite out of their minds; still more so if they had come out of their hiding-places and made trouble for those who controlled the government. Untimely sexual excess, the troublesome manifestation of Christian liberty, had also to be restrained. What, then, does Paul [*(granting that we suppose he is speaking of men who hold public office)*] write to them? Undoubtedly, no new precept but merely those familiar ones, that citizens should be obedient to magistrates, slaves to masters, wives to husbands, and that they were not to think that the yoke of the Lord, however light, frees us from the bonds of duty.[214] Instead, he says we ought to strive more earnestly than before not to neglect anything in the whole range of duties which might contribute to winning men's goodwill by our virtuous behaviour. For only in that way would it come to pass that through us the name of God would be well spoken of among the nations of the world and the glory of the Gospel spread abroad more widely. To achieve this, there was a need for public peace, and its guardians were the princes and magistrates, even if they were evil.

Would you like me to put a clear picture of this before your eyes? Imagine that one of our teachers was writing to Christians living under the Turks, to men, I say, poor in material resources, downcast in spirit, unarmed and few in number, and exposed to every kind of injustice at the hands of all: what other advice would he give, I ask you, than that which Paul gave to the church which then existed at

Rome or which Jeremiah gave to those in exile in Assyria?[215] The surest proof that Paul had in mind those men to whom he was writing, but not all citizens everywhere, is that he scrupulously goes through the mutual obligations of husbands to their wives and of wives to their husbands, of parents to their children and of children to their parents, of slaves to their masters and of masters to their slaves; yet, although he explains what the duty of a magistrate is, he does not (as he had in the earlier cases) address them by name. What are we to believe was the reason which made him refrain from giving any instructions to kings and other magistrates, especially since their passions required the restraint of the shackles of the laws much more than those of private men? What other reason are we to suppose than that at that time there were no kings or magistrates in the church to whom he should write? Imagine Paul was living in our own times when not only the people but princes too profess to be Christians. Let us assume there is at the same time some prince who thinks that divine laws as well as human should be subject to his caprice; who would like not only his decrees but even a nod of his head to be taken as the law; who, as it says in the Gospel, 'neither fears God nor has respect for men';[216] who shares out the revenues of the church among buffoons and jesters – to use no harsher terms; and who mocks the observers of a purer religion and treats them as fools and madmen. What would Paul write to the church concerning such a prince? If he wants to be consistent, he will deny that such a man should regard himself as a magistrate, forbid all Christians to have any food, speech or association with him, leave to the citizens the penalties laid down in the civil laws, and not think they are exceeding their duty if they do not regard as their king a man with whom divine law prevents them from associating.[217]

But someone is sure to be found among our servile courtiers who, since no honourable refuge is available, will carry his shamelessness to the point of saying that God in His anger at peoples sets tyrants over them whom He appoints as executioners to exact punishment.[218] Even if I admit this is true, it is equally true that God frequently stirs up from the lowest ranks of the people humble and obscure men as avengers of the pride and violence of tyrants.[219] For God, as was said before, commands that the evil man be removed from our midst, and He makes no exception of rank, sex, condition or even person, for kings are no more acceptable to Him than beggars. We can truthfully assert, therefore, that God, father of all equally, from whose providence nothing is hidden and whose power nothing can resist, will leave no crime unpunished. Next, another will rise up and demand an example from Holy Scripture of a king being punished by his subjects. Even if I could not produce one, it will not immediately follow that, because we do not find such an act recorded there, it must at once be deemed criminal and impious. I can list from many nations numerous highly beneficial laws for which there is no precedent in Holy Writ. For just as all nations have agreed in accepting that what a law enjoins is to be regarded as just, and what it forbids as unjust, so never in the memory of man has it ever been forbidden to do what is not covered by the law. We have never accepted the servile principle that whatever is not prescribed by some law or handed down in some famous example is to be considered wicked and execrable, and nature, so prolific in new examples, will not allow it to be accepted. So if anyone asks me for an example from the books of Holy Scripture where the punishment of evil kings is approved, I shall ask him in turn where it is censured. If it is agreed that nothing should be done without precedent, how many of our civil processes will be left to us? How many of our laws? Most of them, after all, are not derived from ancient example, but were created to deal with new and unprecedented crimes.[220]

*

But we have now replied at unnecessary length to those who demand precedents. Even if the kings of the Jews were not punished by their subjects, these examples do not have much bearing on our practice.

For they were not originally elected by their subjects but were given to them by God, and He who founded the office for them had every right to inflict punishment as well.[221] We, however, maintain that the people, from whom our kings derive whatever rights they claim, are more powerful than kings, and that the populace at large has the same rights over them as they have over individuals in that populace. All the laws of other peoples who live under legitimate kings support our case; all nations who obey kings elected by themselves share the view that a people can for just causes demand back from anyone whatever rights it has given him. Every commonwealth has retained this right at all times. Thus Lentulus was compelled to resign his praetorship because he had conspired with Catiline to overthrow the Republic;[222] the decemvirs, who framed the laws of Rome, were deposed although they held the highest magistracy;[223] some of the doges of Venice, as well as Chilperic, King of the Franks, laid down the symbols of authority and spent their old age as private individuals in monasteries;[224] and not so long ago Christian, King of the Danes, ended his life in prison almost twenty years after being deprived of his kingdom.[225] Even the office of dictator, which was a kind of tyranny, fell within the power of the people.[226] This law has always been observed, namely, that public favours ill-bestowed might be reclaimed, and that freedom, which the law particularly supports, can be taken away from ungrateful freedmen.[227] This is the sum of what I have to say about foreign countries, to show that we alone have not adopted an unprecedented right over our kings. As for what directly applies to us, the matter can be dealt with in a few words.

M. How? I am eager to hear that.

B. I could go over the names of a dozen or even more kings who were either condemned to lifelong imprisonment for their crimes and scandalous behaviour or who escaped the just penalty for their crimes by exile or suicide.[228] But in case anyone complains that I am bringing up old and obscure cases if I recall kings like Culen, Evenus and

Ferchard,[229] I shall put forward a few from within our fathers' memory. All the estates passed judgement in a public assembly that James III had been justly slain because of his extreme cruelty to his subjects and his scandalous infamy, and they decreed that none of those who had combined, conspired and contributed money or assistance should suffer for it in the future. [230] In deciding after the event that the action was right and proper, there is no doubt that they wanted to establish it as a precedent for the future. This is no less true of L. Quinctius who, in open court, praised Servilius Ahala for butchering Sp. Maelius in the forum when he turned his back and refused to come to court; and he did not think that Servilius was polluted with the blood of a citizen but ennobled by the killing of a tyrant, a view supported by every succeeding generation.[231] If he approved of the killing of a citizen who was striving to make himself a tyrant, what do you think he would have done in the case of a tyrant engaged in robbing his subjects of their goods and shedding their blood? What about our own countrymen? In passing a public decree granting immunity to those who had carried out the deed, do they not seem to you to have established a law dealing with that action if it ever recurred in the future?[232] In the end, it makes no difference whether you pass judgement on an action which has taken place or make a rule on a future action. Either way a judgement is made on the type of deed and the reward or punishment appropriate to its author.

M. Your views will perhaps carry weight among our countrymen, but I do not know how they will be received abroad. You see, I must satisfy foreigners, not on a criminal charge, as if in a court of law, but in the eyes of the world on a point of reputation – not my own (for I am far removed from any suspicion), but that of my fellow-countrymen.[233] I am afraid that foreign nations are likely to lay more blame on the principles by which you think you are sufficiently protected than on the actual deed, full though it was of barbarity and hatred. As for the precedents which you have put forward, I am sure you know what is usually said for and against them according to each man's wit and judgement. I should like you (since you seem to me to have explained everything else on the basis not so much of human laws as of natural principles) to expound briefly anything you have to say for the equity of that law you mention.

B. Although it may seem unfair to plead before foreigners in defence of a law which has from the very earliest days of the Scottish kingdom been approved by the usage of so many centuries, a law which is essential to the people and neither unjust nor dishonourable to our kings, and only now attacked as unconstitutional,[234] nonetheless for your sake I shall attempt the task. And as if I were debating with the very men who will seek to cause you trouble, I first of all ask you this question: what is there here which you think merits censure? Is it the reason why the law was required, or the law itself? It was required in order to restrain the unjust passions of kings. Anyone who condemns this ought to condemn just as energetically all the laws of every people, for they were all required for the same reason. Or do you criticise the law itself and think it fair that kings should be above the laws? Let us see whether that is advantageous too. I need few words to show that it is not beneficial to the people at least. For if in our earlier discussion we were right to compare a king with a physician, then just as it is not to the people's advantage that the physician should be allowed to kill with impunity anyone he wishes, so it is not in the public interest that kings should be granted indiscriminate licence to plunder everyone. We have no reason then to be angry with the people, in whom lies supreme power to make law, if, just as they want to be ruled by a good king, so they want a king who is not of the best to be ruled by the law. But if this law is not to the king's advantage, let us see whether we should negotiate with the people over the question of their relinquishing some part of their right; and let us call an assembly to consider the repeal of that law, not twenty-four days from now, but, according to our own custom, on the fortieth day.[235] Meanwhile, to debate the same matter here between ourselves, tell me, if someone releases a madman from confinement, do you think he is taking account of the madman's interest?

M. Not at all.

B. What about the person who gives a cold drink to a patient who keeps asking for it but is so ill with fever that he is not far from being mad? Do you think he is doing the sick man a service?

M. But I am speaking about kings in their right minds, and I deny that men in sound health need medicine, or that kings in their right minds need laws. You on the other hand want all kings to be thought of as evil, for you impose laws on them all.

B. I do not think all kings are evil, by any means. But neither do I believe the people as a whole to be evil, and yet the law addresses them all with one voice. Now the evil dread that voice, while the good think that it has nothing to do with them. Thus good kings have no reason to resent this law, and wicked kings, if they had any sense, would be grateful to the law-maker who ordained that they should not be allowed to do something which he understood would be disadvantageous to themselves. They will certainly be grateful if they eventually regain their sanity, just as those who are relieved of a disease give thanks to the physician whom they hated for not giving in to their desires when they were sick. But if kings persist in their madness, the person who defers to them most deserves to be judged their greatest enemy. In this category are sycophants who, by indulging the vices of kings with flattery, aggravate the disease and generally in the end themselves plunge headlong to destruction along with the kings.[236]

M. I certainly cannot deny that such princes have deserved and still deserve to be restrained by the chains of the laws. For there is no more violent and more destructive monster than man when, as in the stories told by poets, he has once degenerated into a beast.[237]

B. You would say this much more emphatically if you considered how complex a creature man is and how he is composed of various monsters. The poets of old discerned this clearly and expressed it elegantly in relating how Prometheus, in forming man, brought together in him some small particle of every living thing.[238] It would be an interminable task to describe each of their natures one by one, but certainly two hideous monsters are clearly visible in man, anger and lust. And what else do the laws do or seek to do but to subject these monsters to reason and to restrain them by the fetters of the law's own commands if they do not submit to reason? Whoever, then, releases the king, or anyone else, from these bonds does not simply set a single man free, but lets loose against reason two monsters, by far the cruellest in existence, and equips them to break through the restraints of the laws. Hence it seems to me that Aristotle spoke rightly and truly when he said that the man who obeys the law obeys God and the law, but the man who obeys the king obeys a man and a beast.[239]

M. Although these arguments seem neatly enough expressed, I think we have made a double error. Firstly, because what has just been said does not appear to me to be entirely consistent with our earlier discussion; and secondly, because, even if our other arguments are consistent, we do not seem to have made any real progress towards the point of our debate. We agreed earlier that the voice of the king and of the law ought to be the same, but now we make the king subject to the laws. Even if we grant that this is absolutely right, what precisely have we gained by this conclusion? For who will call to account a king who has become a tyrant? [*Who will prosecute him? Or if the defendant refuses to appear, who can force him or exact compensation or a fine from him?*] I am afraid that right without might will not be strong enough by itself to restrain a king who forgets his duty or to drag him into court against his will to stand trial.

B. I am afraid you have not paid proper attention to our earlier discussion of royal power. If you had, you would have easily understood that those points which you have just made are not mutually inconsistent. So that you can grasp this more easily, first answer me this: when a magistrate or clerk dictates a form of words to a herald, is not the voice of both of them the same – I mean the herald and the clerk?[240]

M. Exactly the same.

B. Which do you think is more important?

M. The one who dictates the form of words.

B. What about the king who is the author of the edict?

M. He is more important than either of them.

B. With this likeness in mind, then, let us compare the king, the law and the people. The voice of the king and of the law is the same. Which of them derives authority from the other? The king from the law, or the law from the king?

M. The king from the law.

B. What leads you to that conclusion?

M. Because the king was not required to restrain the law, but the law to restrain the king; and he derives from the law the very fact that he is a king, for without the law he would be a tyrant.

B. The law, then, is more powerful than the king and is, as it were, the guide and governor of his desires and actions.

M. That has already been conceded.

B. Well then, is not the voice of the people and the law the same?

M. Yes, the same.

B. Which is the more powerful, the people or the law?

M. The people, I think, taken as a whole.

B. Why do you think that?

M. The people are, as it were, the parent, or at any rate the author, of the law, since they can make or repeal it as seems appropriate.

B. Since the law is more powerful than the king, therefore, and the people more powerful than the law, let us see whether there is anyone before whom we can summon the king to stand trial. Likewise let us examine this question: are not things which are established for the sake of something else of less value than those for whose sake they were required?

M. I should like you to put that more clearly.

B. Follow it this way, then: was not the bridle devised for the sake of the horse?[241]

M. Yes, for the horse, of course.

B. What about saddles, trappings and spurs?

M. For the same reason.

B. And if there were no horse, there would be no use for these things.

M. None.

B. The horse, then, is more important than all these things.

M. Of course.

B. What about the horse? For what use is it wanted?

M. A great many, but particularly for gaining victory in war.

B. Do we, therefore, place a higher value on victory than on the horses, arms and everything else which is made ready for use in war?

M. Certainly.

B. In appointing a king, what above all did men have in mind?

M. The advantage of the people, in my opinion.

B. And if no human society existed, there would be no need for kings?

M. None at all.

B. The people, therefore, are superior to the king.

M. It must be so.

B. If they are superior, they are also greater. When the king is summoned before a court of the people, then, the lesser is summoned to stand trial before the greater.

M. But when shall we hope for such good fortune that the whole body of the people agrees as to what is right?

B. That is, I admit, scarcely to be hoped for. Nor, indeed, need we wait for it to happen, otherwise no law could be passed and no magistrate appointed. For there is almost no law which is really fair to everyone, and almost no one who has such popular favour that nobody is hostile to him or jealous and critical of him. The aim is simply that the law should be advantageous to the greater part of the people and that the greater part of the people should have a favourable opinion of the candidate. So if the greater part of the people can pass a law and elect a magistrate, what is to prevent them judging a magistrate themselves or appointing judges to try him? Or if the Roman tribunes of the people and the Spartan ephors were required in order to mitigate the force of authority, why should it seem unjust to any man if a free people have provided themselves in a similar or even in a different way with the means of restraining the harshness of tyranny?[242]

M. I think I am now close to understanding what is in the power of the people, but it is difficult to judge what they might want or propose. The greater part of the people generally look for what is old and familiar, and shrink from novelty. This is all the more remarkable in view of their great fickleness over food, dress, buildings and the entire range of furnishings.

B. Do not think that I have said these things because I want something new to be done in this type of case. I said what I did in order to show that it was ancient practice that a king should stand trial before judges, even though you believed it to be not merely novel but almost incredible. For, to pass over how often this happened among our ancestors, a matter which we have to some extent gone over earlier and which you can easily gather from history, have you ever heard of those who were competing for the kingship appealing to arbiters?

M. I have heard that this sometimes happened at least among the Persians.[243]

B. Our writers relate that the same thing was also done by Grim and Malcolm II.[244] But in case you object that judges of this type are usually engaged by litigants with their own consent, let us come to the ordinary judges.

M. I am afraid that here you are doing much the same as someone who casts a net in the ocean to catch whales.

B. Why so?

M. Because every arrest, restraint or punishment is carried out by the stronger against the weaker. But who are the judges before whom you will command the king to appear? Before those over whom he himself has the supreme power of judging? Those whom he could control with the single word: I forbid.[245]

B. What if some greater power is found which has the same rights over kings as kings have over everyone else?

M. I am eager to hear your argument.

B. If you remember, we said that this power is vested in the people.

M. In the people as a whole, yes, or in the greater part of them. I make you this further concession: it is vested in those to whom the people or the greater part of the people have transmitted that power.[246]

B. Thank you for saving me that trouble.

M. But you are well aware that the majority of ordinary people are corrupted by fear or rewards or by hopes of bribery and impunity, so that they prefer their own interests and pleasures to the public interest and even common safety. There are not so very many who are not moved by such considerations: 'Few indeed in number are the good. They are scarcely as many as the gates of Thebes or the mouths of the wealthy Nile'.[247] All the rest of the rabble, fattened on blood and booty, envy others their freedom, though they put their own up for sale. Leaving aside those for whom the name even of bad kings is sacrosanct, I pass over as well those who, although they know very well what is permissible and just, prefer peaceful indolence to honourable dangers, and anxiously adjust their plans to fit their expectation of the outcome, or follow a party's fortune, not its cause. You see how numerous this crowd is likely to be.

B. A large number certainly, but not the largest. For the injustices of tyrants can affect many, but their favours concern few. The avarice of the common people is insatiable and, like a fire, it burns all the more fiercely when fuel is added. What is taken from the many by force feeds the hunger of the few, but it does not satisfy their appetite. Besides, the loyalty of such men is generally fickle 'and stands or falls with fortune'.[248] Even if they were especially steadfast in their views, however, they would still not deserve to be reckoned as citizens. For they are the destroyers of human society, or at least its betrayers, a vice which, if it is not to be tolerated in a king, is much less tolerable in a private individual. Who, then, are to be counted as citizens? Those who obey the laws and uphold human society, who prefer to face every toil, every danger, for the safety of their fellow countrymen rather than grow old in idleness, enjoying an ease divorced from honour, and who keep always before their eyes, not their immediate pleasures, but the renown in which posterity will hold them. And although there are those who recoil from danger out of fear or regard for their own interests, yet the splendour of a noble action and the beauty of virtue will raise dejected spirits, and those who will not venture to take the initiative or to lead will not hesitate to be followers. So if citizens are reckoned, not by number, but by worth, not only the better part but also the greater will stand for freedom, honour and security.[249] Even if all the common people disagree, that has no bearing on our present discussion, for the question facing us is not what is likely to happen but what can rightfully be done. But now let us go back to the ordinary courts.

M. For some time now I have been waiting for that topic.

B. If some private individual maintains that his estate or some part of his land is being held unfairly by the king, what do you think he should do about it? Will he give up his land since he will not be able to bring a case against the king in court?

M. Not at all. He will instruct the king's attorney, not the king, to appear in court.

B. Consider now the effect of that defence which you are using. It makes no difference to me whether the king himself appears in court or his procurator. In either event the king will be at risk in the litigation: any profit or loss arising from the result of the trial will fall to him, not to his procurator. In short, the king himself is the defendant, that is, the person whose case is in dispute. I would like you now to consider not only how absurd but also how unjust it is that judgement can be given against the king over a small estate, over light for a building, or over rain-water dripping from the eaves of a house,[250] but no case can be brought over parricide, poisoning, or treason. In lesser matters, the full severity of the law is applied, while the most shameful crimes are given the greatest licence and impunity, so that ancient saying seems to be quite true, that 'the laws are very like spiders' webs, which catch flies but let larger creatures through'.[251] There is no justification, either, for the complaint and protest of those who argue that it is neither proper nor just that a verdict on a king should be delivered by a man of lower rank. After all, they see this practice already accepted in a suit about money or land, and men of the highest rank after the king generally defend themselves before judges who are not their equals in wealth or birth or achievements; men whose standing is not so very far above the common people and who are much more inferior in rank to the defendants than men of the highest rank are to kings. Yet these aristocrats and leading men do not think that their standing has thereby suffered any loss. But if we once accept the notion that no one can be brought before a judge unless the judge is superior to him in all respects [*and not just in legal authority*], those of humbler rank will have to wait until the king has either the inclination or the leisure to hear a case involving a nobleman.

Besides, the complaint of those you mention is false as well as unjust. For no one who comes before a judge comes before an inferior, especially since God Himself pays so much honour to the judicial order that He calls them not only judges but gods and, so far as this is possible, imparts to them His own dignity.[252] Those Roman pontiffs, therefore, who graciously allowed kings to kiss their feet, who sent their own mules to them as a mark of honour as they approached, and who trampled on the necks of emperors,[253] would obey when summoned to a court of law and resign their office when compelled to by the judges. When John XXII was brought back from flight and even thrown into prison, and only with difficulty finally ransomed, he knelt in homage before another who was chosen to replace him, and by that homage he gave his approval to the verdict of the judges.[254] What of the Synod of Basle? Did it not resolve and decree with the general consent of all estates that the pontiff was subject to a senate of priests? You can find out from the acts of the council what the arguments were which persuaded those fathers to do this.[255] I do not see, then, how kings, who admit that the majesty of pontiffs rises so far above themselves that it overshadows them all by its exalted height, can believe that their own dignity is diminished when they are in a position to which a pontiff did not think it an indignity to descend from a throne so much the higher – namely, to plead his cause before the council of cardinals. [256]

You see how false is the complaint of those who are offended at being summoned before a tribunal of their inferiors? For in legal cases it is not some Titius or Sempronius or Stichus who condemns or acquits,[257] but the law itself, which those most distinguished emperors, Theodosius and Valentinian, declared it honourable for kings to obey. Since their words so deserve to be remembered in every age I shall add them here: 'It is (they said) an utterance worthy of a ruler's majesty for a prince to admit that he is bound by the laws, and in truth to submit one's rule to the laws is greater than power to command. And by the present solemn edict we declare what we do not allow as lawful to another.'[258] This was what the best of princes believed and enacted, and even the worst understood it too. For Nero is said to have dressed up like the lyre-players, not only adopting their gestures and movements, but when the time came for the judges' verdict standing between hope and fear, uneasy over victory. Although he knew that he would be declared the winner, he thought that his victory would bring him more honour if he obtained it in a proper contest and not because the judges flattered him. By observing the rules, he believed he was adding to the brilliance of his victory, not weakening his authority.[259]

M. What you say is, I see, not as extraordinary as I had thought at first, when you wanted kings to obey the laws, for it rests less on the authority of philosophers than on that of kings, emperors and councils of the church. But I do not quite follow you when you say that it is not a man but the law which passes judgement.

B. Recall for a moment what we agreed earlier. We said, did we not, that the voice of the king and of the law is the same?

M. We did.

B. What about the voice of the clerk and of the herald when he proclaims the law?

M. They have the same voice.

B. What about the judge's voice when he applies the law in his decisions?

M. The same again.

B. Which of them derives his authority from the other, the judge from the law, or the law from the judge?

M. The judge from the law.

B. The force of the verdict, then, comes from the law. The judge merely utters the words.

M. So it seems.

B. In fact nothing is more certain. The verdicts of judges are valid when pronounced in accordance with the law, otherwise they are rescinded.

M. Absolutely right.

B. You see, then, that the judge has his authority from the law, not the law from the judge.

M. Yes, I do.

B. And the lowly rank of the person pronouncing the verdict does not diminish the dignity of the law, but the dignity of the laws is always the same, whether it is a king or a judge or a herald who pronounces the verdict.

M. Absolutely.

B. Once the law has been enacted, then, it is first the voice of the king and then the voice of others.

M. Yes.

B. It seems, therefore, that when a king is condemned by a judge, he is condemned by the law.

M. Quite so.

B. If he is condemned by the law, then, he is condemned by his very own voice, since the voice of the law and of the king is the same.

M. By his own voice, so it seems, no less than if he were condemned by documents written in his own hand.

B. Then what reason do we have for worrying so much about the judge when we possess the king's own confession, that is, the law? Why not also look into this point which has just occurred to me? When the king sits in any case as a judge, should he not lay aside all other roles, of brother, father, kinsman, friend, enemy, and retain only the role of judge?

M. Yes, he should.

B. And he should keep in mind that one role which is appropriate to the case?

M. I should like you to put that more clearly.

B. Listen, then. When someone secretly seizes the property of someone else, what do we say he is doing?

M. Stealing, I think.

B. What name do we give him on account of this action?

M. Thief, of course.

B. What of someone who sleeps with another man's wife as if she were his own?

M. We say he is committing adultery.

B. What shall we call him?

M. An adulterer.

B. What of the man who judges?

M. We call him a judge.

B. And the rest can be given their proper names in this fashion from the actions which they are carrying out at the time.

M. Yes, they can.

B. When the king administers justice, then, he will put aside all other roles.

M. Certainly he will, and particularly those roles which can harm one or other of the litigants in the making of a judgement.

B. What about the man whose case is being judged? What name shall we give him from his activity?

M. We can call him the defendant.

B. And it is fair, is it not, that he should lay aside those roles which can interfere with the trial?

M. Certainly any roles he may play other than that of a defendant are of no concern to the judge, since God does not wish that account should be taken even of the poor man when a judgement is made.[260]

B. Then if someone who is a painter and a grammarian is involved in a court case over the art of painting with someone who is a painter but not a grammarian, his knowledge of grammar ought not to benefit him?

M. No.

B. Nor should his skill in painting benefit him if the case concerns grammar?

M. No more than before.

B. In the trial, then, the judge will recognise only one name, that is, of the crime of which the defendant is accused by his opponent.

M. Yes, that alone.

B. What if a king should be accused of parricide? Is the name of king of any consequence to the judge?

M. No, only that of parricide; for he has come to deal with a dispute over parricide, not over the kingdom.

B. What if two parricides are brought to trial, one a king, the other a poor man? The judge will try them both in the same way, will he not?

M. In the very same way; and Lucan seems to have spoken with no less truth than elegance when he said: 'On the banks of the Rhine Caesar was my general, here he is my partner: crime levels those whom it pollutes.'[261]

B. That is certainly true. In this case, then, judgement will be passed concerning parricides, not concerning a king and a poor man. If the question were which of the two ought to be king, or if the issue were whether Hiero is a king or a tyrant,[262] or if any other issue were to arise which properly relates to the function of a king, then judgement would be passed concerning the king, just as the trial would be about the painter if the question were whether he has any knowledge of the art of painting.

M. What if the king refuses to come to court of his own accord and cannot be compelled by force to do so?[263]

B. His position is the same as that of all criminals, for no robber or poisoner will come voluntarily to court. But you know, I imagine, what the law allows: a thief may be killed at night in any circumstances, but in daytime only if he defends himself with a weapon.[264] But if he cannot be brought to trial except by force, you remember what usually happens then. We pursue by war and force of arms robbers too powerful to be dealt with by the law. The pretext generally given for all wars between nations, peoples and kings is injustices, which, when they cannot be settled by law, are decided by the sword.

M. Admittedly wars are usually waged against foreign enemies for such reasons. With kings the position is different, since we are bound in obedience to them, pledged by the most sacred oath.

B. We are indeed bound by oath; but they on their part promise first that they will administer justice on the basis of what is right and good.

M. That is so.

B. There is, therefore, a mutual pact between a king and his subjects.

M. So it seems.

B. The one who first goes back on the accord and acts contrary to what he has agreed makes the pact and agreement void, does he not?

M. He does.

B. If the tie which bound together the king and the people is broken, therefore, any right belonging to the one who broke the pact is, I think, forfeited.

M. Yes, it is forfeited.

B. Also the person with whom the agreement was made becomes as free as he was before the agreement.

M. Clearly he enjoys the same right and the same freedom.

B. Now if a king acts in ways which break up the human society which he was appointed to hold together, what do we call him?

M. A tyrant, I think.

B. But a tyrant not only possesses no just authority over the people, but he is also the enemy of the people.

M. Undoubtedly.

B. A war against an enemy on account of grievous and intolerable wrongs is a just war?

M. Clearly a just war.

B. What about a war waged against an enemy of the whole human race, that is, against a tyrant?

M. That is the most just of wars.

B. Now when a war has once been undertaken against an enemy for a just cause, it is the right not only of the people as a whole but also of individuals to kill the enemy?

M. I admit it.

B. What about the tyrant, the public enemy, with whom all good men are constantly at war? Cannot any individual from the whole mass of the human race lawfully exact from him all the penalties of war?

M. I think that almost every nation has held that view. Thebe is commonly praised for killing her husband, Timoleon for killing his brother, Cassius for killing his son, Fulvius for putting to death his son who was setting out to join Catiline, and Brutus for putting to death his sons and kinsmen when he learned that they had conspired to restore the tyrant.[265] Rewards and honours for the killers of tyrants were established at public expense by many of the Greek cities, such was their belief, as has already been said, that they had no bond with tyrants, not even the bond of humanity.[266] But why do I cite individual instances of approval when I can produce the testimony of almost the entire world? Who does not severely censure Domitius Corbulo for having so little regard for the safety of the human race that he failed to depose Nero when he could easily have done so? He was criticised not only by the Romans but by the Persian king, Tiridates, who feared nothing less than that this precedent might some day apply to himself.[267] But even the minds of the worst of men, brutalised by cruelty, are not so devoid of this general hatred of tyrants but that sometimes it bursts out against their will and compels them to stand in numb amazement before a picture of truth and virtue. When the servants of that most cruel of tyrants, C. Caligula, men whose cruelty equalled his, were in an uproar at the killing of their master and demanded the execution of those responsible, crying out again and again, 'Who has killed the emperor?', Valerius Asiaticus, a man of consular rank, cried out from a conspicuous place where he could be both seen and heard, 'If only I had killed him'. At these words men who had lost almost all humanity appeared thunderstruck and ceased their uproar.[268] So great is the strength of virtue that when the faintest semblance of it comes to mind violent emotions abate, frenzied excitement subsides, and madness acknowledges the authority of reason, willy nilly. Nor do those who now move heaven and earth with their outcry think differently. We readily see this, if only in the fact that those who condemn what has been done in the present circumstances,[269] praise and approve the same actions or apparently worse ones when these are recited from ancient history. Whereby they openly show that they are more moved by private inclinations than disturbed by any public injury. But why do we seek a better witness of what tyrants deserve than their own conscience? That is the source of that constant fear of everyone and especially of good men: they see always hanging over their own necks the sword they keep forever unsheathed against others, and they measure the attitude of others towards them by their own hatred of other men.[270] Good men, on the other hand, often create danger for themselves by being afraid of no one, weighing the goodwill of others towards themselves, not by men's vicious nature, but by their own service to others.

B. You think it true, then, that tyrants should be reckoned among the most savage of beasts, and that tyrannical violence is more unnatural than poverty or disease or death or all the other evils which can befall men in the natural course of events?

M. For my part when I consider the weight of the arguments I cannot deny the truth of what you say. But when the dangers and disadvantages which follow from this view occur to me, somehow my mind is immediately checked, as if a bridle had been thrown over it, and it turns away from that excessively Stoic and rigid notion of right towards expediency and almost gives in. For if anyone at all is allowed to kill a tyrant, see what an opening for villainy you leave to wicked men, how great a danger you create for the good, how much licence you allow the bad, and what wholesale chaos you set loose on everyone. Who will fail to cloak his crime in that semblance of virtue you afford when he kills a good king or at least a king who is not the worst? Or if someone from the ranks of good citizens either attempts in vain to kill a prince meriting every kind of punishment or even succeeds in carrying out the deed he has planned, how much general disorder must inevitably ensue. While the bad will be in an uproar, furious at the removal of their leader, not all good men will approve the deed, and not all of those who do will defend the author of their liberty against a wicked faction. Most of them will hide their inactivity behind the honourable pretext of peace, or misrepresent the courage of others rather than confess their own cowardice. Assuredly, this recollection of private advantage, this justification of their desertion of the public cause, this fear of danger – all these might at least weaken, if they do not break, the spirit of most men, compelling them to prefer tranquillity, however insecure it might be, to the uncertain expectation of freedom.

B. If you remember what we said earlier, this fear of yours will be easily dispelled. For we agreed that there are certain forms of tyranny sanctioned by a free vote of the people, and we consider these worthy of the name of kingship because of the moderation of their rule. No one will have my support if he uses violence not only against any rulers of this kind but even against any of those who have gained power by force or fraud, provided that they have shown themselves to be temperate and public-spirited in their government. Among the Romans Vespasian, Titus and Pertinax were men of this kind, among the Greeks Alexander, and at Syracuse Hiero.[271] Although they gained power by force of arms, they earned by their just and fair behaviour the right to be considered lawful kings. Besides, under this heading I am explaining what legitimately may or should be done; I am not issuing a call to action. In the former case it is sufficient to describe the facts and give a clear explanation; in the latter, good counsel is needed in forming a plan, prudence in undertaking it, and courage in bringing it to fulfilment. These requirements are helped or hindered by considerations of time, person, place and everything else involved in carrying out the action. So if anyone attempts it rashly, the blame for his mistake does not attach to me any more than a doctor who has properly prescribed remedies for diseases should bear the blame for someone who has given them to patients at the wrong time.

M. It seems to me one thing is still needed to complete this discussion. If you supply it, I shall consider that you have put the finishing touch to the favour I have received from you: I mean if you enable me to understand what is the church's view on tyrants.

B. You can find it for yourself whenever you wish in Paul's first Epistle to the Corinthians, where the Apostle forbids them to share in any meal or conversation with those who are openly wicked or scandalous.[272] If this were observed among Christians, the wicked would have to perish of hunger, cold and exposure unless they came to their senses.

M. That opinion carries great weight, of course, but I wonder whether the people, who are everywhere accustomed to make so much of magistrates, will believe that kings also should be included under this rule.

B. Certainly the older ecclesiastical writers without exception took this interpretation of Paul's opinion. Ambrose excluded the Emperor Theodosius from the company of Christians, and Theodosius obeyed the bishop.[273] Nor, so far as I know, has the action of any bishop won higher praise in antiquity, nor the modesty of any emperor been more highly commended. But for our purpose, how much difference does it make whether you are driven out of the Christian community or are prohibited from using fire and water?[274] For the latter is the most severe sentence imposed by all magistrates on those who refuse to obey their commands, and the former the most severe imposed by ecclesiastics. In either case the penalty for treating authority with contempt is death, but the one commands the destruction of the body, the other the destruction of the whole man. Will not the church, therefore, which believes that much less serious offences should be punished by death, consider that death is deserved by the man whom in life it expels from the company of the good and in death banishes to the company of devils?

*

I think that I have said all that the justice of our case requires. If it fails to please some foreigners, I ask them to reflect how unfairly they treat us. Since there are numerous great and wealthy nations throughout Europe, each with its own laws, those who prescribe for everyone else their own form of government are behaving arrogantly. The Swiss have a republic, Germany enjoys a lawful monarchy, though it is called an empire, and some cities in Germany are, I hear, subject to the nobility; the Venetians have a government which is a mixture of all these, and Muscovy delights in a tyranny. Our kingdom is small, I admit, but now for 2,000 years we have held it in freedom from rule by foreign peoples.[275] We have appointed lawful kings from the beginning, and have established laws which are fair both to us and to them. The long passage of time shows their value, for this realm has endured to this day less by arms than by the observance of these laws. What injustice is this that they should want us to repeal or disregard laws whose value we have tested through the experience of so many centuries? What impudence is this that those who can scarcely protect their own authority should try to overthrow the form of government of another kingdom? Need I add that our institutions are of value to our neighbours as well as to ourselves? After all, what can be more valuable for maintaining peace between neighbours than the restraint of kings? For it is commonly as a result of their uncontrolled desire that unjust wars are recklessly begun, wickedly prosecuted, and dishonourably abandoned. Furthermore, what is more harmful to any commonwealth than for its neighbours to have bad laws from which infection often spreads more widely? Or why are we the only ones they pester, when so many nations around and about use different laws and institutions, none being exactly the same? Or why is it only now that they pester us, seeing we are not establishing anything new but are adhering strictly to an ancient law? And seeing we are not the only people nor the first to adopt these practices, and this is not the first time that we have made use of them? But our laws displease some people: perhaps their own laws displease them too. We do not go prying into the practices of other peoples, so let them leave us with our own, tested by the experience of so many years. Do we interfere with their councils? In what way, I ask, do we pester them? But you are rebels, they say. I might reply frankly, 'What has that to do with them? If we are in uproar, ours is the danger, ours the damage.' I could list a great many insurrections which have not been harmful to commonwealths and kingdoms. I shall not make use of that defence. I maintain that no people is less prone to insurrection, that none has been more moderate when insurrections occur. There have been many disputes over the laws, over the right to wield authority, over the government of the kingdom, but always the things that matter most have remained intact. Our struggles have not involved, as they have with most peoples, the ruin of the common people or hatred of our princes, but instead a love of country and a zeal to defend our laws. How often within our memory have great armies faced each other ready for battle, and how often have they disengaged not only without anyone being wounded but even without any harm or altercation?[276] How often has the public interest calmed private quarrels, and how often has a report of the approach of a foreign enemy put an end to domestic feuds? But in our insurrections also our good fortune has equalled our restraint, since on nearly every occasion the party which had more justice on its side has also been the more successful; and just as we have pursued our domestic feuds with restraint, so we have duly reached an amicable agreement.

These are the thoughts occurring to me at present which might seem capable of silencing the gossip of the malicious, refute the more stubborn, and satisfy the more fair-minded. I have not, however, considered it of much importance to us what the laws of kingship are in other countries. I have explained our own practice briefly, but at greater length than I had planned or than the subject required, because I undertook this task for you alone. If it meets with your approval, I am satisfied.

M. As far as I am concerned, you have fully satisfied me, and if I can likewise satisfy others I shall feel that I have profited greatly from this discussion and gained relief from an extreme irritation.

The End

The Stoic King from Seneca[277]

Neither worldly wealth nor robes of Tyrian purple make a king, nor a crown upon a princely brow nor halls gilded with gold. A king is one who has laid aside fear and the torments of an evil conscience, who is not moved by uncontrolled ambition and the fickle favour of the reckless mob, or by all the treasure mined in the West, or the golden waves that sweep down Tagus' glittering bed, or all the grain threshed on the burning Libyan plain. He is one who is not shaken by the hurtling path of a slanting thunderbolt, or by the east wind harrying the sea, or the violent waves of the raging Adriatic's windswept swell; who is not subdued by a warrior's lance or an unsheathed sword; who, removed from harm's way, sees everything before him and gladly hastens to meet his fate, grieving not to die.

Although kings may assemble who torment the scattered tribes of Scythia, who hold sway by the shore of the Red Sea with its blood-red waves sparkling with jewels, who defend the Caspian pass from bold Sarmatians; though he vies with one whose feet dare tread the icebound Danube and they (wherever they are) who cast down the silk farms of the noble Chinese – it is a noble mind that masters a kingdom. There is no need for horses or arms, or the cowardly darts that the Parthian hurls from afar as he pretends to flee; no need of war machines hurling rocks to flatten cities. A king is he who fears nothing; [a king is he who desires nothing.] Such a kingdom each man gives himself.

The End

Notes and Commentary

[1]   Buchanan expends little effort on establishing the setting and circumstances in which his conversation with Maitland took place. The preliminaries are confined almost exclusively to introducing the subject matter of the debate that is to follow. Maitland probably did return to Scotland from France in 1567, but he subsequently denied participating in any such dialogue with Buchanan.

[2]   Various writers in antiquity discussed the influence of climate on character, but Buchanan is drawing here on Aristotle, *Politics*, VII, vii, 2 (1327b). Sixteenth-century Scots were particularly keen to assert that, despite their northerly location, they were no less civilised than other peoples.

[3]   The 'crime' referred to here is, of course, the murder of Henry Stewart, Lord Darnley, on 10 February 1567.

[4]   As becomes clear, the 'recent crime' to which Maitland is now referring, and for which the *Dialogue* offers a defence, is the deposition of Mary for her alleged involvement in her husband's murder.

[5]   Here, as throughout the *Dialogue*, Buchanan simply assumes Mary's complicity in her husband's murder.

[6]   Thomas Maitland's brother, Sir William Maitland of Lethington, the queen's former secretary, was deeply implicated in the events surrounding Mary's abdication in 1567.

[7]   The great Periclean age of Athens came to an end with the outbreak of the Peloponnesian War (431-404 BC) between Athens and Sparta. Both Pericles and his wayward relative Alcibiades are the subject of biographies by Plutarch, and Buchanan appears here to be building on an anecdote in Plutarch, *Alcibiades*, vii, 2.

[8] Buchanan's is presumably referring to the religious wars that tore France apart in the 1560s and 1570s, but his Latin here is unusually obscure and the precise meaning of the sentence is unclear.

[9] Horace, *Epistles*, I, i, 39-40.

[10] The Roman emperors Caligula (AD 37-41), Nero (AD 54-68) and Domitian (AD 81-96) were by-words for tyranny, and Nero and Caligula in particular are frequently referred to by Buchanan.

[11] That is, his assent to the proposition that the killing of tyrants is lawful. The idea of a lawful – and thus irresistible – tyranny is one to which Buchanan returns later in the *Dialogue*.

[12] An echo of the opening lines of Homer's *Odyssey*, I, 3: 'He saw the cities of many peoples and learnt their ways.'

[13] Compare the similar claim to impartiality made by Tacitus in the opening chapter of his *Annals*, I, i, 3.

[14] This marks the end of the preliminaries that serve to introduce the subject of the *Dialogue* and the parameters of the subsequent discussion. This is structured (as Buchanan has suggested) in terms of an analysis of kingship and its opposite, tyranny, to each of which is devoted approximately half of the text. Buchanan begins his treatment of kingship by embarking on an analysis of the origins of social organisation and the reasons for the creation of kings; this is followed by a lengthy discussion of the need to subject rulers to the authority of the law – in many respects, the main point of the *Dialogue* – culminating in a description of the 'ideal king'.

[15] This probably owes something to Cicero, *De Inventione*, I, ii, 1: 'For there was a time when men wandered at large in the fields like animals and lived on wild fare; they did nothing by the guide of reason, but relied chiefly on physical strength; there was as yet no ordered system

of religious worship nor of social duties; no one had seen legitimate marriage nor had anyone looked upon children whom he knew to be his own; nor had they learned the advantages of an equitable code of law.' Cicero goes on to attribute social and political association to the power of eloquence and the orator – a view that Buchanan will shortly and explicitly reject.

[16]   The passage from Homer, *Odyssey*, IX, 112-15, relates to the Cyclopes. It is referred to in Aristotle, *Politics*, I, ii, 7 (1252b), in the course of a discussion of the origins of human association, and quoted in full in Plato, *Laws*, 680b.

[17]   The fertility of Italy is eulogised in Virgil, *Georgics*, II, 136-76, and assessed more soberly in two Greek works: Strabo's *Geography*, VI, iv, 1, and Dionysius of Halicarnassus' *Roman Antiquities*, I, xxxvii. Note again Buchanan's awareness that Scotland was at some distance from the heart of civilisation.

[18]   Buchanan is here combining lines from two classical poets: firstly, from Horace, *Satires*, I, iii, 98, where in the course of an attack on orthodox Stoicism, Horace gives the sort of utilitarian account of the origins of society associated with the Epicureans; and secondly, from Juvenal, *Satires*, XV, 157-8.

[19]   An echo of Cicero, *De Officiis*, I, vii, 22: 'But since, as Plato has admirably expressed it, we are not born for ourselves alone, but our country claims a share of our being, and our friends a share; and since, as the Stoics hold, everything that the earth produces is created for man's use; and as men, too, are created for the sake of men, that they may be able to help one another ...'. Cf. Plato, *Epistle IX*, 358a.

[20]   See Homer, *Iliad*, VI, 200-3. Bellerephon was a Corinthian hero who survived various attempts on his life by his enemy, Proetus, before being abandoned by the gods and driven into solitude. Timon was a famous Athenian misanthrope of the time of Pericles.

21   A slightly modified version of Ovid, *Metamorphoses*, I, 76-8.

22   Juvenal, *Satires*, XIV, 321.

23   A reference to Matthew, xxii, 37-40.

24   Buchanan here rejects the view advanced in Cicero, *De Inventione*, I, ii, 2-3, that an orator (Cicero does not specify a lawyer) was responsible for human association in ordered communities, though ironically he immediately goes on to assert the divine origins of society on the authority of another work by Cicero.

25   Buchanan is paraphrasing Cicero, *De Republica*, VI, xiii, 13. Although a complete text of *De Republica* was not available in the sixteenth century, the part known as *Scipio's Dream*, where this passage occurs, was preserved embedded in the commentary of the shadowy fifth-century Neoplatonist, Macrobius, and was highly popular throughout the Middle Ages and the Renaissance.

26   Horace, *Epistles*, I, i, 82.

27   Here Buchanan introduces an analogy between the king and a physician which, much favoured by Aristotle and Plato, is more fully exploited as the *Dialogue* progresses. The suggestive metaphor of the body politic, again deriving from classical sources, was commonplace by the sixteenth century, as was the theory, associated with the second-century Greek physician, Galen, that the body was composed of 'humours' and 'temperaments' whose balance in the individual determined personality.

28   Aristotle, *Politics*, III, xiii, 13 (1284a) refers to such a man – 'so greatly superior to others in goodness and political capacity' – as 'a god among men'. Elsewhere, and more frequently, he refers to him as 'the best of men' or 'the one best man'. There is an obvious affinity here with the 'philosopher-king' of Plato's *Republic* and perhaps in

particular the perfect ruler – 'the divine shepherd' – of his *Statesman*, 275b-c, 276d.

[29] For references to 'father Aeneas', see Virgil, *Aeneid*, I, 699; V, 348. For Agamemnon as 'shepherd of the people', see Homer, *Iliad*, II, 243, and Aristotle, *Ethics*, VIII, xi (1161a).

[30] Cf. Plato, *Republic*, 345c-e; the same idea underlies the contrast between a king and a tyrant (frequently echoed by Buchanan) in Aristotle, *Politics*, V, x, 8-10 (1310b-1311a).

[31] The king-doctor analogy, dove-tailing so neatly with the metaphor of the body politic, is common in classical writings, and Plato in particular made extensive use of it in the *Republic*, the *Statesman* and, to a lesser extent, the *Laws*. While it is hard to find exact parallels, the form and substance of the argument that follows is almost certainly indebted to the *Statesman* in general and to 293a-296e in particular.

[32] The virtues to which Buchanan is referring are the four cardinal virtues – wisdom, temperance, fortitude and justice – made so much of in the political and ethical writings of Aristotle and Plato. The function of reason and the virtues in restraining man's baser instincts – his passions – lies at the heart of Buchanan's understanding of kingship and tyranny, and draws heavily on Plato in particular.

[33] For this and what follows, see Aristotle, *Politics*, III, xiii, 25 (1284b), but particularly Plato, *Statesman*, 301d-e. See also on beehives and the 'king' bee, Seneca, *De Clementia*, I, xix, 2-3; and more generally on 'political organisation' among bees, Pliny, *Natural History*, XI, iv-xxiii.

[34] See Aristotle, *Politics*, III, xvi, 2-3 (1287a), for the likely source of this argument.

[35] Buchanan's Latin, echoing Livy, V, i, 3, might be translated more pejoratively as 'weary of the annual scramble for office'.

[36]   An adaptation of Cicero, *De Oratore*, II, viii, though Buchanan may also have in mind Aristotle, *Rhetoric*, I, i, 1-2, where the function of an art is said to be the discovery of a particular system or method. However, the argument that Buchanan now pursues, comparing the art of government with other arts, contains much that is reminiscent of Plato, *Statesman, passim*.

[37]   Like Plato and Aristotle, Buchanan recognises the impossibility of realising this ideal and thus the necessity of government by laws. As becomes clear, however, unlike Plato or Aristotle, Buchanan is not prepared to allow the ruler any latitude in the interpretation or administration of the law.

[38]   Terence, *Self-Tormentor*, 483.

[39]   Buchanan evidently shared the common sixteenth-century view of Venice as a model republic. James VI is alleged to have told the Venetian ambassador to England in 1603 that Buchanan had instructed him in the excellence of Venice's constitution; that he did not convince his pupil is suggested by the king's remarks on 'the Duke of Venice' in the *Trew Lawe of Free Monarchies* (see *Minor Prose Works*, p. 73).

[40]   Buchanan's reference to the authority of laws being more powerful than that of men echoes Livy, II, i, 1. His admiration for Venice and (republican) Rome is obvious; the more obscure and oligarchic government of the city-state Massilia or Massalia (Marseille) is mentioned in Aristotle, *Politics*, V, vi, 2-3 (1305b), and Strabo, *Geography*, IV, i, 5.

[41]   Buchanan was a great admirer of Spartan kings and kingship, though like his classical authorities (Plato, Aristotle, Xenophon, Plutarch) was actually less interested in the persistence of Sparta's unusual dual kingship than in the other restraints on the essentially military authority of the kings represented by such institutions as the ephorate.

[42] Cf. Livy, II, i, 7, on the appointment of consuls for a year.

[43] Buchanan's Latin echoes the famous Roman law formula from Digest, I, iii, 31: 'The prince is not bound by the law' (*Princeps legibus solutus est*). Variations on the phrase occur frequently in the *Dialogue*, which is, in many respects, intended as a refutation of the absolutist sentiments which it could be construed as embodying.

[44] Cf. Aristotle, *Politics*, III, xv, 5 (1286a): 'That from which the element of passion is wholly absent is better than that to which such an element clings. Law contains no element of passion; but such an element must always be present in the human mind.' Aristotle, however, was much less convinced than Buchanan that the ruler must be subject at all times to the authority of the law.

[45] An adaptation of *De Legibus*, III, i, 2, where Cicero refers to magistrates rather than kings: '... the function of a magistrate is to govern, and to give commands which are just and beneficial and in conformity with the law. For as the laws govern the magistrate, so the magistrate governs the people, and it can truly be said that the magistrate is a speaking law, and the law a silent magistrate.'

[46] The 'most renowned' historian is, of course, Livy, though this is a rather sly borrowing from part of a self-serving defence of kingship by the Tarquins, in which they claimed that, if kings were expelled in the name of liberty, all order would collapse (II, ix, 3).

[47] Presumably a reference to Lucius Quinctius Cincinnatus who, according to Livy (III, xxvi, 7-9), was working on his little farm – 'bending over his spade as he dug a ditch, or ploughing' – when he was summoned to become dictator at Rome. However, Buchanan may also have in mind how David was summoned from the pastures where he was shepherding his flock and was anointed by Samuel at God's command (I Samuel, xvi, 11-13).

⁴⁸ Here again Buchanan is drawing on Livy, III, xxvi, 7: 'What follows [i.e., the summoning of Cincinnatus] merits the attention of those who despise all human qualities in comparison with riches, and think there is no room for great honours or for worth amidst a profusion of wealth.'

⁴⁹ The story was a common one in the classical world, but Buchanan's most likely source is Plutarch, *Moralia*, 179c-d, ('Sayings of Kings and Commanders', 31).

⁵⁰ Agesilaus reigned in Sparta from 398 BC until his death in 360. Buchanan's enthusiasm may derive from the biography of him in Plutarch's *Lives* or from Xenophon's *Agesilaus*. Leonidas I reigned from 490 BC until his death, in a heroic last stand against the Persian armies of Xerxes, at the battle of Thermopylae in 480, fully described in Herodotus, VII, 201-33.

⁵¹ Gorgo was the daughter of Cleomenes, king of Sparta from c.509 BC to 490, and wife of Leonidas I. The source of this particular anecdote is Plutarch, *Moralia*, 240e ('Sayings of Spartan Women', 3). Buchanan's knowledge of the 'domestic habits' of Spartan kings more generally would have been derived from such works as Xenophon's *Constitution of the Spartans* and Plutarch's account of the reforms of Lycurgus (c.800 BC) in his biography, *Lycurgus*.

⁵² Juvenal, *Satires*, VI, 3-4.

⁵³ Pelagius or Pelayo, a Visigothic nobleman, won a minor victory over Moorish forces at the battle of Covadonga in 717/8 and established an independent Christian kingdom in the Asturias (north-west Spain, including Galicia) where he reigned until 737. Unimportant in itself, his defeat of the Moors became in subsequent historiography a key moment in the reconquest of Christian Spain. By Buchanan's time the kings of Castile traced their ancestry back through Pelayo to the Emperor Theodosius and Theodoric the Ostrogoth.

[54] Cicero is referring to Herodotus, I, 96, which recounts how the Medes chose Deioces as their sole judge because of the fairness of his decisions.

[55] Cicero, *De Officiis*, II, xii, 41-2.

[56] Buchanan probably has in mind the contrasting portraits of tyranny and kingship in Xenophon's *Hiero* (tyrant of Syracuse 478-467 BC) and *Agesilaus* (joint king of Sparta 398-360 BC) as well as the *Cyropaedia*, where Cyrus the Great (founder of the Persian empire) is presented as an ideal king.

[57] In fact, as we have already seen, Buchanan makes extensive use of both Plato and Aristotle in the *Dialogue*. Although they applied the principle much less stringently than Buchanan, both believed that, in the absence of an ideal king, the ruler must be subject to the law.

[58] Either Buchanan or his publisher helpfully appended the relevant lines from Seneca's *Thyestes* to printed editions of the *Dialogue*.

[59] The often gruesome customs of the Scythians, nomadic peoples of the Ukrainian steppes, are described in detail in Herodotus, IV, 59-75.

[60] A reference back to Pericles in Athens, Spartan kings such as Agesilaus and Leonidas, and Philip of Macedon.

[61] Moses was persuaded by his father-in-law, Jethro, to choose others to judge less important cases on his behalf, while he himself retained jurisdiction over more important ones. Exodus, xviii, 14-26.

[62] Cf. *Digest*, I, i, 1-2: '... in terms of Celsus' elegant definition, the law is the art of goodness and fairness. Of that art, we [jurists] are deservedly called the priests.'

[63] Aristotle, *Politics*, III, xv, 6 (1286a): 'There is, however, a whole class of matters which cannot be decided at all, or cannot be decided properly, by rules of law.' Aristotle proceeds to enunciate a principle of equity (*epieikeia*) residing in the person of the ruler in a manner that Buchanan was unwilling to accept. Plato, *Statesman*, 294a ff., pursues a similar line of argument to Aristotle, exploiting the analogy between the doctor and the king in a manner that has distinct echoes here.

[64] Cf. Plato, *Statesman*, 295d, 296b.

[65] Buchanan is reshaping Livy, II, iii, 4, but see also Plato, *Statesman*, 294b-c, where the law is described as 'an obstinate and ignorant tyrant, who will not allow something to be done contrary to his appointment, or any question to be asked'.

[66] Buchanan here recalls the attack by Horatius' father on the inflexibility of the law which would condemn his son to death in Livy, I, xxvi, 6-11. The same formula can also be found in Cicero, *Pro Rabirio*, IV, 13. The Roman 'lictor' was the official who attended upon a magistrate and who was charged with executing sentence upon convicted offenders.

[67] Compare Aristotle, *Politics*, III, xvi, 7 (1287b), on the same theme.

[68] A remarkably forced and inapposite application of Romans, ii, 14, where Paul is not referring to an ideal ruler.

[69] A reference back to the discussion of the 'one best man', whose superiority renders him 'a god among men', in Aristotle, *Politics*, III, xiii, 13-14 (1284a), and to Aristotle's conclusion: 'There can be no law which runs against men who are utterly superior to others. They are a law in themselves.'

⁷⁰ Buchanan is expressing a view associated with the Stoics, and found, for example, in Cicero, *De Natura Deorum*, I, xiv, 36, and Seneca, *De Beneficiis*, IV, vii, 1.

⁷¹ The idea of the soul imprisoned in the body was something of a classical commonplace, but Buchanan's argument as it develops here is once again reminiscent of Plato, *Statesman*, 301d-e.

⁷² Compare Leviticus, xix, 15.

⁷³ Terence, *Phormio*, 501.

⁷⁴ An echo of Galatians, iii, 23-4.

⁷⁵ The quotation is from Virgil, *Aeneid*, I, 5; however, the rest of the sentence suggests Roman comedy, where city slaves are often threatened with banishment to their masters' country estates, or, worse still, with being sent to work in the mill: see, e.g., Terence, *Lady of Andros*, 199.

⁷⁶ Horace, *Epistles*, I, i, 76. The phrase was a commonplace by the sixteenth century.

⁷⁷ Buchanan's use of the Greek term *probouleuma* ('preliminary resolution') suggests that he had in mind the ancient Athenian system where the popular assembly (*ekklesia*) of some 40,000 citizens elected a smaller council (*boule*) of 400 (later 500), which both acted as a standing committee of the *ekklesia* and was responsible for preparing motions and resolutions (*probouleuma*) for its consideration. Buchanan's knowledge of it probably derived from the brief account in Plutarch, *Solon*, xix, 1-2.

⁷⁸ As becomes clearer later in the *Dialogue*, the idea of conflict between reason and the passions in the human soul, a doctrine common in classical antiquity but fundamental to Stoic moral and political

philosophy, lies at the heart of Buchanan's conception of kingship and tyranny.

[79] Here and in what follows, Buchanan is clearly influenced by Aristotle, *Politics*, III, xi, 1-2 (1281a-b), and III, xv, 7-8 (1286a).

[80] Mithridates the Great, King of Pontus (120-63 BC), was thought to have safeguarded himself against poison by taking small amounts of various harmful substances beforehand. Pliny, *Natural History*, XXIX, viii, 24, claims that his antidote was made from fifty-four ingredients.

[81] An allusion to Aristotle's celebrated doctrine of 'the mean'; see in particular *Ethics*, II, vi-ix (1106a-1109b).

[82] The use of this theme in Roman schools is mentioned in both Cicero, *De Oratore*, II, xxiv, 100, and Quintilian, *Institutio Oratoria*, IV, iv, 4. Elsewhere in the latter, however, in a passage on which Buchanan appears to be drawing here, Quintilian explores more fully the inequity of applying the full rigour of the law to a foreigner who has scaled the walls *in defence of* the city (VII, vi, 6-7).

[83] See Cicero, *De Officiis*, I, x, 33: 'Injustice often arises also through chicanery, that is, through an over-subtle and even fraudulent construction of the law. This it is that gave rise to the now familiar saw: "More law, less justice"'. The phrase, which is extremely hard to translate, was still proverbial in the sixteenth century. Buchanan's pupil, James VI, in the *Trew Lawe of Free Monarchies*, was to insist on the grounds of the same axiom that kings must be permitted to override the law should the interests of their subjects so dictate (see *Minor Prose Works*, p. 72).

[84] Cicero, *De Legibus*, III, iii, 8.

⁸⁵ Buchanan is presumably referring to the rules of forensic oratory, to which so much of the writings of classical authorities on rhetoric, such as Cicero and Quintilian, were devoted. His words might be interpreted pejoratively as an attack on lawyers and their oratorical tricks, but this is the line taken by Maitland in the following speech, and it seems likely that in this instance Buchanan is approving of the use of the rules of rhetoric as a means of regulating court-room disputes between advocates.

⁸⁶ Buchanan is referring to a mason's rule, made of lead, which could be bent to fit the curves of a moulding; hence its subsequent proverbial meaning of a pliant principle or law. He may well have in mind Aristotle, *Ethics*, V, x (1137b).

⁸⁷ Buchanan is referring here to the principle of Roman law that in cases concerning a person's status the judge is expected to start from the presumption that the defendant is a free person. To illustrate this principle a colourful but unhistorical tale was told (*Digest*, I, ii, 2 (24)) of the killing of the maiden Verginia by her father in order to save her from Appius Claudius, portrayed as the benevolent *decemvir* turned tyrant, who claimed that Verginia was a slave rather than a free woman in order to circumvent the law. The story is told in detail in both Livy, III, xliv-xlix, and Dionysius of Halicarnassus, *Roman Antiquities*, XI, xxviii-xxxix.

⁸⁸ As will become clear, Buchanan has in mind I Timothy, iii, 1-4.

⁸⁹ This is the first of several attacks on the more extreme pretensions of the medieval papal monarchy – the 'fullness of power' possessed by 'the vicar of Christ' – associated with such popes as Gregory VII (1073-85), Innocent III (1198-1216) and Boniface VIII (1294-1303).

⁹⁰ In fact, it was the Merovingian king, Childeric III, who was removed from office by the hereditary mayor of the palace, Pippin or Pepin the Short. Pippin appealed to Pope Zacharias for support,

who famously argued that it was better to recognise as king the person who possessed power rather than he who did not. Pippin was formally installed as king of the Franks in 751, while Childeric (as Buchanan later notes) retired to a monastery where he died in 755.

[91]   Presumably a reference to the conquest and annexation of the kingdom of Navarre by Ferdinand ('the Catholic') of Aragon in 1512. Navarre was then in French hands, ruled by Jean d'Albret and his wife Catherine de Foix, and Ferdinand accused the Navarrese rulers of being schismatic for their support of the Council of Pisa, summoned by the French king, Louis XII, in defiance of Pope Julius II. In 1513, at Ferdinand's behest, Julius II issued a bull of deposition (though its authenticity has been questioned), while subsequent Spanish propaganda upheld the papal deposing power.

[92]   Henry, Count of Luxembourg, was elected king of Germany in 1308 and crowned Holy Roman Emperor as Henry VII at Rome in 1312. The following year, despite being threatened with excommunication by Pope Clement V, he marched his army south to attack Robert, King of Naples. When he died of a fever on the way, his supporters claimed he had been given poison in the sacramental wine by a Dominican friar acting on the pope's behalf.

[93]   I Timothy, iii, 2. In what follows, it is unlikely that Buchanan has any particular pope in mind; the idea of the bishop being married to his diocese was a medieval commonplace.

[94]   Again, Buchanan is unlikely to have a particular pope in mind. Rather he is parodying papal attitudes to pluralism. Innocent III at the Fourth Lateran Council of 1215 had outlawed the practice, though with the proviso that 'exalted and lettered persons' might be exempted (*Decrees of the Ecumenical Councils*, I, pp. 247-9). The ban was reiterated in even stronger terms at the seventh session of the Council of Trent in March 1547 (*ibid.*, II, p. 687). Subsequently,

however, at Trent's twenty-fourth session in November 1563, it was recognised that these earlier decrees had proved less than effective. The Council once again decreed, therefore, that all ranks of churchmen, including cardinals, should hold only one benefice, though here too provision was made that 'if this does not suffice to support the incumbent in a reasonable fashion, another simple benefice may be granted him provided that both do not require residence' (*ibid.*, II, pp. 769-70).

[95] Buchanan is presumably referring to cases so serious that only some higher authority, in some instances only the pope himself, was entitled to pass judgement and grant absolution.

[96] See Dio Cassius, *Roman History*, LIX, xiv, 7, and Suetonius, *Caligula*, lv, 3.

[97] Dio Cassius, *Roman History*, LIX, xxviii, 5-6, recounts how Caligula built a new temple where he would be worshipped as Jupiter Latiaris (hence Buchanan's sarcastic reference to the 'Roman Jupiter' in his next speech), and where he 'consecrated himself to his own service and appointed his horse a fellow-priest'.

[98] Pope Julius III (1550-55) earned notoriety by appointing a street urchin as the keeper of his ape, having him adopted by his brother as Innocenzo, and promoting him aged seventeen to the cardinalate. Buchanan refrains from adding further to contemporary speculation as to the nature of their relationship – whether they were lovers or whether Innocenzo was Julius' son.

[99] See *Digest*, I, ii, 2 (49), where it is said that, from the time of Augustus (27 BC-AD 14), the opinions of certain jurists were to carry the authority of the emperor. Before that time, although the written opinions of distinguished jurists played an important role in the development of Roman law, they were accorded no formal status.

[100] Maitland presumably has in mind here the emperor's role as judge rather than legislator, and his power to issue writs and pass judgements (which, depending on the case, might or might not establish binding precedents) as set down in *Institutes*, I, ii, 6. The problem of the source and extent of imperial sovereignty, deriving from the *lex regia* (*Digest*, I, iv, 1-4; *Institutes*, I, ii, 6) is touched on later in the *Dialogue*.

[101] There may be some substance to Buchanan's point in that, even following Augustus' ruling that the written opinions of certain jurists should carry the authority of the emperor, it was not clear that they were binding on a judge. In practice, however, *pace* Buchanan, they would have been hard to ignore and do appear to have been taken as possessing binding force. The possibility that this might give rise to conflicting (but in theory equally binding) opinions was partially addressed in Justinian's *Institutes*, I, ii, 8, where it was stated that, if the jurists' were unanimous in their views, 'their opinion had such weight that a judge could not depart from the terms of their answer'.

[102] Here, and in what follows, Buchanan combines references to Scottish and Roman legal forms and practice. In Roman law, *praevaricatio* was applied to collusion between the parties to a case, an offence encouraged by reliance on private prosecution in criminal cases. However, when he offers to defend Maitland for nothing, he ignores Roman usage, for strictly speaking a Roman advocate was not permitted to charge for his services. When he goes on to refer to the 'ordinary judges', he intends the term in its Scottish sense of judges of first instance (the baron in a barony court, the magistrate in a royal burgh, the sheriff elsewhere), while the 'council' is the privy council, which still retained in Buchanan's day many of its judicial functions.

[103] A return to Roman usage: banishment to a remote desert island was the Roman penalty for grave offences, often accompanied by financial sanctions (see *Digest*, XLVIII, xxii).

[104] Again, the term *calumniando*, bringing a false accusation, is being used deliberately here in its Roman-law sense, a counterpart to *praevaricare*.

[105] The hint of an essentially Aristotelian contrast between a king and a tyrant, pursued in more detail later in the *Dialogue*, effectively brings to a close what has been a lengthy discussion of the need to subject the ruler to the law. Buchanan now proceeds, after some brief preliminaries, to what is the climax of the first half of the *Dialogue*: a description of the 'ideal king' where, in keeping with the preceding argument, the emphasis is palpably placed on his moral worth to the community rather than his governmental function.

[106] While there had been earlier bans on hereditary succession to ecclesiastical benefices, such as that of the Second Lateran Council of 1139, Buchanan is probably referring here to chapter 7 of the decrees of the twenty-fifth session of the Council of Trent, December 1563 (*Decrees of the Ecumenical Councils*, II, p. 788). To this was added (Chapter 15) the provision to which Buchanan goes on to refer, forbidding the sons of clerics from holding 'any benefice, even a dissimilar one, in churches where their fathers occupy or previously occupied any ecclesiastical benefice, nor serve in these churches in any way, nor hold pensions from the revenues of benefices which their fathers occupy or have occupied elsewhere' (*ibid.*, II, pp. 793-4).

[107] A loose rendering of Terence, *Eunuch*, 353.

[108] Claudian, *Panegyric on the Fourth Consulship of the Emperor Honorius*, 294-302.

[109] *Ibid.*, 272-5. In the sentence immediately preceding the quotation, Buchanan is paraphrasing the immediately preceding lines of Claudian, *ibid.*, 269-71. The phrase 'in the world's stage' was a classical trope: cf. Cicero, *Verrine Orations*, V, xiv, 35, and Curtius, *History of Alexander*, IX, vi, 21.

[110] The allusion to 'a collection of shepherds and strangers' recalls Cicero, *De Oratore*, I, ix, 37; but this and the following sentence owe their substance and phraseology primarily to Livy, I, xxi, 2-3.

[111] In later Roman legend Numa was seen as a second founder of Rome whose contribution to the establishment of religious institutions matched Romulus' achievements in war. According to Livy (I, xviii, 1), the source of Buchanan's account, he was of Sabine origin.

[112] See Numbers, xxi, 8-9.

[113] An adaptation of Livy, III, liv, 3.

[114] A further reference to the lines from Seneca's *Thyestes* appended to the *Dialogue*.

[115] On the king as 'the image of God', see Plutarch, *Moralia*, 780e ('To an Uneducated Ruler'): 'Now justice is the aim and end of the law, but law is the work of the ruler, and the ruler is the image of God who orders all things.' The theme is developed in Erasmus, *Adages*, I, iii, 1, and in his *Education of a Christian Prince*, p. 219.

[116] Horace, *Odes*, IV, iv, 33-4.

[117] Horace, *Satires*, II, i, 32-4. In antiquity it was common practice to erect a dedication to a god if a prayer was granted; vivid pictures put up by sailors saved from shipwreck must have been a familiar sight (see Cicero, *De Natura Deorum*, III, xxxvii, 89).

[118] In what follows, Buchanan is drawing on the story that only Helen's phantom went to Troy with Paris, while the real Helen went instead to Egypt to be looked after by King Proteus. This version of the tale is referred to in Plato, *Republic*, 586c, but Buchanan, the translator of Euripides' plays, *Medea* and *Alcestis*, was probably familiar with it from the same author's *Helen*.

[119] Renowned (and rival) painters of the fourth-century BC, associated with the courts of Philip of Macedon and Alexander the Great. They are frequently mentioned together in later classical literature: e.g., Cicero, *Brutus*, xviii, 70; Cicero, *Letters to Atticus*, II, xxi, 4; Petronius, *Satyricon*, 83.

[120] Persius, *Satires*, III, 35-8.

[121] This marks the beginning of the second part of the *Dialogue* which, focusing on tyranny and the remedies available to a people subjected to tyrannical rule, falls into four distinct sections. In the first, Buchanan pursues the contrast between a king ruling according to law and a tyrant who ignores it, while in the second the focus is on how such tyrants may be restrained in a country such as Scotland where the monarchy is hereditary rather than elective. The third section represents something of a digression in which Buchanan responds at length to scriptural arguments in favour of obedience and non-resistance to tyranny; but in the fourth (and longest) section he returns to his main theme, setting out the natural law principles which legitimise resistance and tyrannicide and on which the Scottish constitution is said to be founded.

[122] Here, and in the discussion that follows, Buchanan displays a humanist's characteristic sensitivity to language and the changing meaning of words. However, as will become clear, his definition of tyranny owes a considerable debt to the seminal analysis in Books III and V of Aristotle's *Politics* as well as to the characterisation of the tyrant as an irrational animal subject to his base passions and appetites in Books VIII and IX of Plato's *Republic*.

[123] Jupiter (Zeus) is referred to as a tyrant in Aeschylus, *Prometheus Bound*, 736, and Aristophanes, *The Clouds*, 564. In early Greek the word tyrannos (derived from eastern sources) did not necessarily have pejorative connotations, though its Latin usage is more usually

hostile. Ovid, *Metamorphoses*, I, 276, and V, 508, refers respectively to
Neptune and Pluto as tyrants.

[124] Suetonius, *Tiberius*, i, 2, tells us that the name Nero in the Sabine
language meant 'strong and vigorous'. It was seldom used after the
Emperor Nero's time. Judas is the Greek form of the Hebrew Judah
(Yehuda); revered in the Jewish tradition, it was for Christians
associated with the betrayal of Christ by Judas Iscariot.

[125] The Latin for 'hangman' (*carnifex*) might mean murderer as well
as executioner. According to Cicero, *Pro Rabirio*, v, 15, 'the censors'
regulations are so framed as to cut off such a man not merely from
using the Forum but from beholding our horizon, breathing our air
or living in our city'. The hangman was in effect a 'public slave'.

[126] The memory of the excesses of the Tarquins left the Romans
with a determination never again to use the title *rex* (king) at Rome.
At the end of the Republic, after the assassination of Julius Caesar in
March 44 BC, P. Dolabella became consul along with Mark Antony,
who had held the consulship since the beginning of the year. Antony
proposed and carried a measure that the dictatorship should be
abolished forever. Despite their vast powers, Augustus and his
successors never assumed the title *dictator*, just as they never
contemplated taking the title *rex*.

[127] With the exception of *scrofa* (the Latin for 'sow'), the etymologies
of these surnames remain obscure. Camillus was the heroic figure
who freed Rome from the Gauls in 387-6 BC (Livy, V, xix, 2ff), but
according to Macrobius, *Saturnalia*, III, viii, 5-7, the Etruscans had
called Mercury 'Camillus', by which they meant 'the attendant of
the Gods'. Metellus has been doubtfully derived from a Greek word
meaning a hired servant, but was lent distinction by Q. Metellus
Macedonicus (d. 115 BC), who made Macedonia a Roman province
in 148 BC. The surname Scrofa was made famous by Gnaeus

Tremillius, praetor and proconsul in Transalpine Gaul in the first century BC who also features in Varro's *De Re Rustica* both because of his cognomen and because he had himself written a work on agriculture.

[128] Kings of Germany as well as Holy Roman Emperors were frequently named Henry (Heinrich), while Charles (Karl), recalling Charlemagne, was equally popular. Genseric (Gaiseric) was a king of the Vandals and the Alani (428-477) who conquered a large part of Roman Africa and sacked Rome itself in 455. Their origins as lower status names remain obscure and the subsequent popularity of Genseric may be doubted.

[129] Aristotle, *Politics*, III, xiv, 8-9 (1285a), IV, x, 2-3 (1295a), in the course of analysing 'legitimate tyranny', discusses the nature of the power held by certain rulers in archaic Greece, called in Latin *aesymnetae*, who were tyrants in their unlimited power but had been installed by election. However, in linking the Greek *aesymnetae* with the Roman *dictatores*, Buchanan may be drawing on Dionysius of Halicarnassus, *Roman Antiquities*, V, 73, whose discussion of the origins of the Roman dictatorship – 'in reality an elective tyranny' – draws explicit parallels with the older Greek institution. The Roman dictator was at first appointed for a period limited to six months and to deal with a specific emergency. The dictatorships of Sulla and Caesar were not limited in this way and it was this development that caused the office to fall into disrepute.

[130] Buchanan is here echoing Justinian, *Institutes*, I, i, 3: 'The commandments of the law are these: live honourably, harm nobody, give everyone his due.'

[131] See, e.g., Aristotle, *Politics*, V, x, 9-10 (1310b-1311a) and his subsequent discussion of 'the arts' by which a tyrant maintains himself in power: *Politics*, V, xi, 1-17 (1313a-1314a); but see too the description of a tyrant in Plato, *Republic*, 565-592.

[132] Perhaps a reference to Hiero II, tyrant of Syracuse in the third century BC, but Buchanan is more likely to be thinking of Hiero I, who reigned at Syracuse from 478 to 467/6 BC. Plutarch, *Moralia*, 551f., enlarges on his virtuous behaviour after his initial seizure of power by force, while in Xenophon's *Hiero* the tyrant is made to participate in an imaginary dialogue in which he argues that a despot is less happy than a private citizen and measures are suggested for gaining the affection of his subjects and thus achieving happiness for himself. As duke of Florence, Cosimo di Medici (1519-74) established a contemporary reputation as something of a benevolent despot.

[133] Buchanan is quoting from Sallust's justification of his decision to abandon politics and turn to writing history: *Jugurtha*, iii, 2.

[134] Cf. II Corinthians, ix, 6.

[135] Cf. Suetonius, *Tiberius*, xxxii, 2: '... the part of a good shepherd is to shear his flock, not skin it.'

[136] Quintilian, *Institutio Oratoria*, VIII, vi, 47, attributes the saying to Cicero.

[137] There is perhaps an echo here of Cicero, *Pro Milone*, 53. Certainly, Buchanan shared the disapproving attitude of Cicero and other Roman moralists to extravagant building, seeing it as symptomatic of the luxury that bred moral corruption and vice.

[138] For a tyrant, who 'from being a man become[s] a wolf', see Plato, *Republic*, 565d-566a. Erasmus, *Education of a Christian Prince*, pp. 223-4, 226, characterises the tyrant in similar animalistic terms: 'Now if you are looking for what corresponds to the tyrant, think of the lion, the bear, the wolf, or the eagle, who live by mutilation and plundering, and, since they realize that they are vulnerable to the hatred of all and that everyone seeks to ambush them, confine themselves to steep

crags or hide away in caves and deserts – except that the tyrant outdoes even these creatures in savagery' (p. 226).

[139] As remarked above, banishment to a remote desert island was a common Roman punishment for serious offences. Although often accompanied by financial penalties, Terence, *Phormio*, 978, refers to the wicked being transported to a desert island at public expense. Livy, XXVII, xxxvii, 1-15, describes how in early Rome atonement for prodigies such as monstrous births was sought through putting the live baby in a chest, carrying it out to sea and throwing it overboard (see also XXXI, xii, 5-8). Buchanan may also have in mind here the punishment for parricide as described in *Digest*, XLVIII, ix, 9: 'A parricide is flogged with blood-coloured rods, then sewn up in a sack with a dog, a dunghill cock, a viper and a monkey; then the sack is thrown into the depths of the sea.'

[140] Cf. Erasmus, *Education of a Christian Prince*, p. 231: 'In the past the honours of divinity were accorded to those who had governed well; but there was a law about tyrants, which nowadays applies to wolves and bears, that a reward would be paid from public funds for doing away with a public enemy.'

[141] In Greek and Roman mythology, the Furies were goddesses of vengeance who lived in the underworld and ascended to earth to pursue the wicked; they were frequently invoked in classical literature from Euripides onwards. It is unclear who Buchanan might have in mind among 'our own writers', but his pupil James VI was to discourse learnedly on evil spirits in his *Daemonologie* (see *Minor Prose Works*, pp. 39-45).

[142] The metaphor of the storm-tossed ship, manned by an untrustworthy crew, has an inexact parallel in Plato, *Republic*, 488, the source of many variations on the theme.

143 Dionysius, tyrant of Syracuse, 406-367 BC. According to Cicero, *Tusculan Disputations*, V, xx, 58, the tyrant's daughters were obliged to dispense with a razor and 'singe his hair and beard with red-hot walnut shells'; cf. Cicero, *De Officiis*, II, vii, 25.

144 Timoleon, a Corinthian aristocrat (died c.334 BC), who freed Syracuse and other Sicilian cities from despotism, is described in Plutarch, *Timoleon*, iv, 4-5, as having his brother Timophanes killed after vainly trying to dissuade him from establishing himself as a tyrant in Corinth. In this account, Timoleon stood apart, while others committed the deed; Diodorus, XVI, lxv, 4-6, has Timoleon himself killing his brother.

145 Cicero, *De Officiis*, II, vii, 25, recounts the story of Alexander, tyrant of Pherae (369-358 BC), being murdered by his wife, Thebe, immediately following his reference to Dionysius. There is a more detailed account in Plutarch, *Pelopidas*, xxxv, 3-7.

146 Spurius Cassius, Roman consul in 486 BC, was executed the following year because of fear that he was intent on re-establishing the monarchy. Livy, II, xli, 10-11, is dubious that it was his father who was responsible for his death; Dionysius of Halicarnassus, *Roman Antiquities*, VIII, lxxix, 1-2, also expresses doubt, but gives the full story nonetheless.

147 Having discussed the meaning of tyranny, and drawn a lurid portrait of the tyrant as a ruler swayed by animal passions who lives outwith the legally-defined norms of civilised society, Maitland now draws attention to the fact that the Scottish monarchy is hereditary and that the idea that an elective kingship, bound by the law, may act as a check on tyranny is irrelevant in a context where the will of the ruler has the force of law. This is an 'absolutist' view of the Scottish constitution that Buchanan proceeds to dispute by recourse to a mixture of Roman law, which he takes to embody natural justice, and appeals to Scottish historical precedents.

[148] Maitland is referring to the celebrated *lex regia* as set out in Justinian's *Institutes*, I, ii, 6 (cf. *Digest*, I, iv, 1): 'A pronouncement of the emperor also has legislative force because, by the Regal Act relating to his sovereign power, the people conferred on him its whole sovereignty and authority.' The absolutist gloss which Maitland puts on this, however, had long been challenged by jurists and others who argued that the people's sovereignty was not transferred fully and permanently to the ruler but was merely delegated in a limited and revocable grant of authority.

[149] It is not clear on what exact source Buchanan is drawing here, but for an inexact parallel, see Suetonius, *Caligula*, xxxiv, 2.

[150] See Suetonius, *Caligula*, xxx, 2, and Dio Cassius, *Roman History*, LIX, xiii, 6.

[151] According to Livy, II, viii, 1, the right of appeal to the people was actually established only after the expulsion of the Tarquins and the founding of the republic in 509 BC (cf. *Digest*, I, ii, 16). However, Buchanan has already made reference to an earlier passage in Livy (I, xxvi, 6-11) where Horatius, returning to Rome following his triumph over the Albans, stabbed his sister to death for grieving over the loss of her Alban lover in the battle. Horatius was found guilty of murder, but was persuaded by his father to submit his case to the judgement of the people, whose admiration for him won his acquittal. Buchanan may also have had in mind Seneca, *Epistles*, cviii, 31, where he states unequivocally 'that there was an appeal to the people even from the kings'.

[152] L. Cornelius Sulla (138-78 BC) is generally credited with inaugurating the beginning of the end of the Roman republic. A distinguished general, primarily engaged in military campaigns against Mithridates, King of Pontus, he was also in 88 BC the first Roman general to lead his legions against Rome itself. In 82 BC he occupied the city a second time and had L. Valerius Flaccus pass a

measure that overthrew the republican constitution and made him dictator with the right to continue in office as long as he wished. Sulla used his powers to institute the mass proscription and butchery of his enemies. For a full (and hostile) account of Sulla's dictatorship, see Appian, *Civil Wars*, I, xi, 98ff., but also, and perhaps more pertinently to Buchanan's point here, Cicero, *De Lege Agraria*, III, ii, 5.

[153] Justinian (c.482-565) was eastern Roman emperor from 527 to 565. An austere and disciplined ruler, his greatest passion, aside from religion, was the law. On his instructions, the 1,500 existing books of Roman law were condensed into the fifty books of the *Digesta* ('ordered abstracts'), promulgated in 533 along with the much shorter *Institutiones* ('principles'), essentially a handbook for first year law students. These texts, together with the collection of imperial constitutions, the *Codex*, formed what came to be known as the *Corpus Iuris Civilis*. The influence of this codification of Roman law was immeasurable.

[154] Horace, *Epistles*, I, xvi, 39-40.

[155] Belisarius (500-565) was one of Justinian's most famous generals. His successful campaigns against the Vandals and the Goths, however, aroused Justinian's suspicions that he might seek to become emperor himself and relations between them were frequently tense and occasionally broke down. The image of Belisarius as a heroic figure unfairly treated by Justinian, generally current in the sixteenth century, derives from the sixth-century Greek historian Procopius, who served on Belisarius' staff, and whose *History of the Wars of Justinian* and especially his *Secret History* are heavily biased in the general's favour.

[156] Tribonian, the main architect of Justinian's codification of Roman law, was briefly forced out of public office on charges of corruption. Legal scholars of the Renaissance period, notably Lorenzo Valla and members of the hugely influential sixteenth-century French school of humanist-jurists, had a low opinion of him, accusing him of ruining

Roman law by tampering with pre-existing legal texts and introducing anachronisms, distortions and contradictions.

[157] Early editions of the *Dialogue* run together these two quotes from Juvenal's *Satires*. The first (X, 96-7) occurs in a passage referring to those who want to enjoy the kind of power held by Sejanus before his downfall; the second (IV, 70-1) is from a passage deriding Domitian's self-satisfaction at being told by a flatterer that the turbot now offered to him had actually wanted to be caught.

[158] As noted in the introduction, Buchanan's principal historical source was Hector Boece's *Scotorum Historia* (Paris, 1527), though he also had access to a manuscript copy of Walter Bower's *Scotichronicon*, dating from the 1440s, as well as the *Historia Maioris Britanniae* (Paris, 1521) of his former teacher, John Mair. However, Buchanan's understanding of Scotland's ancient 'elective' monarchy, in which rulers were frequently held to account by their subjects, is both distinctive and tendentious. Moreover, the historical arguments set forth in the *Dialogue* sometimes conflict in detail with those advanced in Buchanan's own *History*.

[159] It is notable that in what follows Buchanan chooses to highlight the Scots' respect for the monarchy and their restraint in the face of tyrannical rule rather than dwelling on the careers of those early Scottish kings who were held to account by their subjects and who in his *History* are used to substantiate his conception of a Scottish monarchy strictly limited by the law.

[160] James I was murdered in the Dominican Friary at Perth on 21 February 1437. Buchanan's portrait of him in the *History*, II, p. 114; X, lviii, which echoes the phraseology used here, follows in the tradition established by Bower, Boece and Mair in being oddly sympathetic to a ruthless monarch who at least some contemporaries considered to be a tyrant; cf. Bower, *Scotichronicon*, VIII, pp. 301ff.; Boece, *Scotorum Historia*, fo. ccclxvii^{r-v}; Mair, *History of Greater Britain*, pp. 364-9.

[161]　James III was killed following the battle of Sauchieburn on 11 June 1488, the culmination of what was the second major noble uprising against him. The myth of his tyrannical rule was already well-developed by the 1560s, but Buchanan gave the events of 1488 a distinctively constitutionalist gloss. Later in the *Dialogue*, he is more explicit on the constitutional significance of a meeting of the Three Estates that declared the king to have been 'justly slain'.

[162]　Following the battle of Flodden on 9 September 1513, there were rumours that James IV had not in fact been killed on the field but had escaped, only to be killed later (or, in another version, to embark on a pilgrimage to the Holy Land). In 1516, Alexander, 3rd Lord Hume, and his brother, were alleged to have been implicated in the king's death and, though this remained unproven, were executed on other charges. Despite what he says here, Buchanan makes clear in his *History* that he set little store by these tales (*History*, II, pp. 258-60, 271-2; XIII, xl-xli, XIV, vii).

[163]　Culen is one of the most colourful and characteristic exemplars of tyranny in Buchanan's *History*. The historical Culen (*Gaelic*: Cuilén mac Illuib) seized the Scottish throne in 966/7 and was himself killed in 971 by Rhiderch, king of Strathclyde, whose daughter he had taken captive and possibly raped. The basis of Buchanan's portrait of him as a debauched and lustful tyrant may be found in Bower, *Scotichronicon*, II, pp. 354-7, and in more elaborate detail in Boece, *Scotorum Historia*, fo. ccxxxii^v, who as well as telling us that Culen's profligate lifestyle led him to contract gonnorhoea also makes the point that the king was summoned to a convention at Scone where the nobility intended depriving him of his authority. Buchanan follows Boece's account (omitting the medical details), but says in the *History* only that the king's murder met with disapproval and not, as is the case here, that the Estates ordered the murderer to be punished (*History*, I, pp. 297-8; VI, xxvi).

[164] Evenus or Ewen III was unknown to Walter Bower, but, according to Hector Boece, was the sixteenth king of Scots. Deposed and imprisoned by the nobility for his sexual excesses and vicious cruelty, he was immediately murdered by a young child who rather than receiving the reward he anticipated for this public service was in turn executed for the crime (*Scotorum Historia*, fo. xxxvi[r-v]). Buchanan in his *History* (I, pp. 172-3; IV, xxi) closely follows Boece's account of the tyrant's degeneracy, deposition by the nobility and condemnation to 'perpetual imprisonment', but his murderer is 'some person' rather than a child.

[165] The idea that Kenneth III (*recte* Kenneth II; *Gaelic*: Cinead mac Maíl Choluim), king of Scots 971-995, attempted to alter the laws of succession in favour of male primogeniture can be found in Bower, *Scotichronicon*, II, p. 369, and is made much of in Boece, *Scotorum Historia*, fos. ccxxxviii[v]-ccxl[r]. However, while the highly theoretical argument that Buchanan presents in what follows suggests that the king and his nobility negotiated a compromise or 'contract' that established hereditary succession only on condition that the powers of the crown were limited by law, in his *History* he adopts a rather more realistic perspective in which the change to the law of succession is effected by force (*History*, I, pp. 306-13, 324-5; VI, xxxvi-xlii, VII, i).

[166] Buchanan is here reverting to Roman law, invoking the famous dictum from *Digest*, XLIII, xvi, 27: 'Cassius writes that it is permissible to repel force by force, and this right is conferred by nature. From this it appears, he says, that arms may be repelled by arms.' Though Buchanan does little more than allude to it, this private-law argument of self-defence was frequently employed by advocates of resistance to tyranny.

[167] Again, the allusion is to Roman law as found in *Digest*, IV, ii, 1: 'The praetor says, "I will not hold valid what has been done under duress."' However, this and the following point may also owe something to Cicero, *De Officiis*, I, x, 32: 'Further than this, who fails

to see that those promises are not binding which are extorted by intimidation or which we make when misled by false pretences? Such obligations are annulled in most cases by the praetor's edict in equity, in some cases by the laws.'

[168] See *Digest*, IV, i, 1-8, which deals with restitution both to those who have been fraudulently deceived (IV, i, 7) and to minors and 'those who have been absent on state business' (IV, i, 6).

[169] As will become clear, Maitland is returning here to Scottish experience, the 'right' granted to kings by the people referring back to Kenneth III being permitted to settle the succession hereditarily in his own family.

[170] Cf. Livy, V, i, 3.

[171] Maitland is reflecting on the murderous family feuding that was a commonplace accompaniment of the kin-based tanistic succession that still prevailed in parts of Celtic Ireland and Scotland in the sixteenth century – a system on which Buchanan will shortly place a very different gloss. In the Ottoman Empire, the succession was likewise not fixed, and it was common practice for a new sultan to assassinate his brothers on coming to power. But perhaps Maitland has in mind the bloody civil war that resulted from Suleiman the Magnificent's attempts prior to his death in 1566 to fix the succession by executing one son and promoting the cause of another.

[172] Cf. *History*, I, pp. 311-12; VI, xlii, where in his account of the disputes over Kenneth III's attempts to change the law of succession, Buchanan raises a series of similar objections to the principle of male primogeniture.

[173] Presumably, Buchanan has in mind Justinian, *Institutes*, II, xvi, 1, where provision is made, through a form of pupillary substitution, for the succession to property of children who are insane.

[174]   See the discussion at the beginning of the *Dialogue* of the origins of society and the 'mutual benefits' that arise from the establishment of commonwealths bound by laws.

[175]   At Sparta the two kings were subject to the supervision of the ephors, five magistrates elected annually. The establishment of the ephorate was attributed by some ancient authorities to Theopompus who reigned c.700 BC. Buchanan is probably drawing here on Aristotle, *Politics*, V, xi, 2-3 (1313a), but the same story is in Plutarch, *Lycurgus*, vii, and was a stock point of reference for sixteenth-century advocates of limited monarchy. However, it was Calvin's endorsement of the Spartan ephorate as a legitimate restraint on monarchical rule, with a contemporary equivalent in assemblies of the Three Estates (*Institutes*, IV, xx, 31), that made it a commonplace among Protestant resistance theorists.

[176]   Buchanan returns to the theme of the (mythical) antiquity and alleged stability of Scottish kingship in a highly rhetorical passage at the end of the *Dialogue*. Scots had long believed that their kingdom was founded in 330 BC and that, unlike France, Spain or England, it had never been conquered by a foreign power or dynasty. Here, as in his *History*, Buchanan seeks to attribute this to the fact that Scottish kings were held in check by laws enforced by patriotic and public-spirited citizens/subjects. The Cimbri, a tribe from North Jutland, were best known in antiquity for their migration southwards in the late second century BC, but were often regarded as the ancestors of the Danes. The belief in the great antiquity of the Danish monarchy was largely due to the success of Saxo Grammaticus' *Gesta Danorum*, originally written in the early thirteenth century and first published in 1514, which traced the monarchy back to its legendary foundation by the eponymous Dan I.

[177]   The same point is made in Buchanan's *History* (II, pp. 601-2; XX, xxxvii). Buchanan may have had in mind the fourteen-man Council

of the Isles that had traditionally met at Finlaggan on Islay to advise
the Lord of the Isles, but such councils were common in Lowland as
well as Highland society.

[178] Buchanan's Latin is somewhat cryptic here, but the context
suggests that what is intended is a contrast between the potential
for abuse when the king has secure possession by hereditary right
and the people's grant of authority as a favour or privilege (*beneficium*)
which can be revoked if the ruler acts tyrannically.

[179] In the *History* (I, pp. 414-15; VIII, xxx), Buchanan correctly dates
Bruce's seizure of the throne and inauguration at Scone to 1306,
indicating a date of composition for the *Dialogue* of c.1566. Buchanan's
account of Balliol's reign in the *History* (I, pp. 392-40; VIII, x-xvii)
suggests that, while he saw John Balliol as the legitimate heir of
Alexander III by hereditary succession, he believed him to have
forfeited his right to rule by paying homage to Edward I of England
against the wishes of his leading subjects. His thinking on this point
was doubtless indebted to the lengthy discussion of the episode in
Mair's *History of Greater Britain*, pp. 209-20.

[180] There are few surviving accounts of the oath sworn by medieval
Scottish kings at their coronations, but such evidence as there is
indicates that, like their French and English counterparts, they swore
to uphold 'the lawis and lovable customs' of the realm. After the
Reformation, a new oath was drawn up for the coronation of James VI
on 29 July 1567, which, taken on his behalf by the Earl of Morton,
bound him *inter alia* to 'rewle the people committit to my charge,
according to the will and command of God, revelit in His forsaid
Word, and according to the lovabill lawis and constitutionis resavit
in this realme, na wayis repugnant to the said Word of the Eternall,
my God'. The oath sworn on the king's behalf differs significantly
from what was proposed by the Kirk two weeks prior to the coronation
where the nature of the relationship between crown and people was

conceived in explicitly contractual terms. The full texts are printed in James VI, *Minor Prose Works*, pp. 130-2.

[181] Buchanan was certainly familiar with the kind of pageantry and political propaganda that accompanied royal entries, and as early as 1539 had celebrated in verse Charles V's triumphal entry into Bordeaux (*Political Poetry*, pp. 258-63). In Scotland as elsewhere, civic authorities used such occasions not just to display their loyalty, but to impress religious and political messages upon the monarch, as when Mary Queen of Scots was welcomed into Edinburgh in September 1561 and pointedly presented with a vernacular Bible and Psalter. However, while such occasions clearly presented opportunities for 'dialogue' between monarch and people, it is less certain that the ceremonials involved the kind of solemn oath-taking implied here by Buchanan.

[182] See I Kings, ii, 4, where David tells Solomon of God's promise to him that, if their descendants remained faithful to Him, they would never lack a successor on the throne of Israel. As one might expect, Buchanan chooses to emphasise the restrictions imposed by God's law rather than the prospect of David's descendants reigning in perpetuity.

[183] The source of this definition remains unclear, but cf. Justinian, *Institutes*, I, ii, 4.

[184] This draws to a close Buchanan's efforts to rebut Maitland's claim that his arguments have no relevance to a monarchy such as Scotland where kings rule hereditarily rather than by election. He now proposes therefore to turn his attention to the key issue of the punishment of kings – or tyrants – who refuse to adhere to the rule of law. At this point, however, Maitland raises the objection that the Bible appears to sanction the view that even tyrants rule by the will of God and may not be resisted. To this Buchanan responds at length with a series of arguments that effectively blunt the universal application of

key scriptural passages by insisting on their relevance primarily to the historical context in which they were written.

[185] Cf. *Digest*, I, iii, 33.

[186] As becomes clear, the passage in question is I Samuel, viii, 1-22, where God responds through Samuel to the people of Israel's request to have a king set over them. The response details the tyrannical regime, characterised by the reduction of the people to servility and servitude and the arbitrary seizure of their goods and property, which their kings would subsequently establish. Nevertheless, the passage concludes, the people would not heed the voice of Samuel, but insisted on being like other nations, having a king set over them who would be their judge and lead them in war.

[187] Buchanan is alluding to a passage in Herodotus (VII, 104) where the tyranny of law or custom is said to compel Spartans to excel others in fighting courageously for their country. More generally, however, the opaque allusion to the 'tyranny of habit' and subsequently to the abandoning of 'the inveterate customs of so many centuries' are more likely to refer to the rejection of Roman Catholic religious practices.

[188] The verses from I Samuel, viii, to which Maitland has drawn Buchanan's attention, were frequently interpreted as supplying scriptural authority for non-resistance to even the most tyrannical of monarchs (e.g., Calvin, *Institutes*, IV, xx, 26). Buchanan's pupil, James VI, agreed and devoted much of his *True Lawe of Free Monarchies* (*Minor Prose Works*, pp. 57-82) to an exposition of the passage.

[189] According to I Samuel, i-iv, Eli was a priest in the house of the Lord whose sons' behaviour was so scandalous that God laid a curse on them and their descendants.

[190] See Aristotle, *Politics*, VII, vii, 2 (1327b), on the servility of Asian peoples.

[191] Buchanan clearly has in mind Deuteronomy, xvii, 18-20, where the kings of Israel are bound to rule according to the laws of God. Erasmus, *Education of a Christian Prince*, pp. 226-7, similarly develops an argument that contrasts the 'ideal prince' of Deuteronomy with the image of tyranny invoked by Samuel.

[192] St Paul is traditionally believed to have been a victim of the persecution of Christians initiated towards the end of the Emperor Nero's rule (54-68). A Jew, but also a Roman citizen, as a young man he was himself an active persecutor of Christians before his encounter with the risen Christ and conversion towards the end of the reign of the Emperor Tiberius (14-37). His subsequent mission to the Gentiles thus spanned the reigns of Nero's immediate predecessors, Caligula (37-41) and Claudius (41-54).

[193] Titus, iii, 1.

[194] I Timothy, ii, 1-2.

[195] Buchanan is referring here specifically to Romans, xiii, 3-4, but in what follows he addresses the issues raised by verses 1-5 as a whole where Paul states that the powers that be are ordained by God and that whoever resist them resists the ordinance of God and will suffer damnation. The passage was of enduring significance for those who advocated strict obedience to the civil powers, while presenting those who wished to argue the case for resistance to tyranny with a serious exegetical challenge.

[196] It has not been possible to identify the source of this quotation. It does not occur where one might expect to find it in Chrysostom's *Homilies on Romans, XXIII* (on Romans, xiii, 1-10), though Buchanan's subsequent argument may well owe something to Chrysostom's highly influential reading of the text.

[197] That Paul was seeking to counter the antinomian tendencies of those in the early church whose extreme understanding of Christian liberty led them to reject all law and civil authority is evident not just in his Epistle to the Romans, but also in those to the Thessalonians, Corinthians and Galatians. Buchanan's argument here was no doubt informed by the commentaries of sixteenth-century reformers, for whom the issue of Christian liberty became crucial in the wake of the excesses of radical sects such as the Anabaptists. Thus Calvin's view of obedience to the temporal authorities was directly shaped by his fear of how Christian liberty might be misconstrued in precisely the way suggested by Buchanan; see especially Calvin, *Institutes*, III, xix ('Of Christian Liberty'), and IV, xx ('Of Civil Government'), and his *Commentary on Romans*, pp. 477-8.

[198] Buchanan is referring here in very oblique terms to a distinction between the office of magistracy and the person of the magistrate to which he will return shortly. It is a distinction highlighted in Chrysostom, *Homilies on Romans*, XXIII, p. 511 ('Nor am I now speaking about individual rulers, but about the thing in itself.') and was to prove crucial in efforts to qualify the apparently absolute nature of the Pauline injunction to obey. While Calvin was reluctant to exploit the distinction (merely alluding to it in his *Institutes*, IV, xx, 22), other reformers were prepared to build on Chrysostom's words, arguing that while the office was divinely ordained and owed unstinting obedience, the holder of the office might well abuse the ordinance of God and might justly be resisted.

[199] Buchanan's views here effectively epitomise the arguments of Calvin, *Institutes*, III, xix, and IV, xx.

[200] Cf. Jerome, *Epistles*, LXIX, 5.

[201] This was certainly true of England, where a statute of 1352 made it treason to encompass the death not just of the king, but also of officials such as the chancellor and treasurer. The Scottish law of

treason was never elaborated on in the same way, though in 1515 Lord Drummond was forfeited for laying hands on the king's herald (*APS*, II, p. 284).

[202] Having developed a distinction between the office of magistracy and the person who holds magisterial office, Buchanan now argues that inferior magistrates must be included among the 'powers' that Paul insists are ordained by God. This argument originated in the constitutional theory of the Holy Roman Empire and was adopted by Lutheran theologians in the 1530s as a means of justifying the resistance of German princes to the authority of the emperor. It was subsequently taken up by a wide range of Protestant resistance theorists, but was perhaps most fully explored by Theodore Beza in his *Du Droit des Magistrats* (1574). However, Buchanan's point here is concerned less with the role of inferior magistrates in resisting authority than with establishing that they too are accountable under the law.

[203] Chrysostom, *Homilies on Romans*, XXIII, p. 512, in putting the case for the necessity of government, concludes: 'For anarchy, be where it may, is an evil, and a cause of confusion.'

[204] This was certainly Calvin's view: see, e.g., his *Commentary on Romans*, p. 477.

[205] See Jeremiah, xxvii, though it is not the king of the Assyrians to whom the Jews are admonished to render obedience, but Nebuchadnezzar, King of Babylon. Buchanan goes on to argue that this example implies no universal precedent, but Maitland's view finds powerful support in Calvin, *Institutes*, IV, xx, 27.

[206] Ahab, King of Israel, fought his final battle against the Syrians at Ramoth-gilead in disguise, having been warned by the Prophet Micaiah that the outcome would be fatal (I Kings, xxii; II Chronicles, xviii). However, though mortally wounded by an archer, there is

nothing in these accounts to indicate either that his killer was rewarded or that, as Buchanan goes on to say, the commander of his own troops was the perpetrator.

[207] See I Timothy, iii, 1-7, for Paul's advice on how bishops should behave. The passage does not, however, contain any comparison with kings such as Buchanan proceeds to develop.

[208] The relationship between temporal and spiritual authority was of course the source of bitter controversy throughout much of the medieval period and was never as straightforward as Buchanan's optimistic, if not ironic, gloss on Paul's words suggests. Papal pretensions, which he proceeds to lambast, reached their height with Boniface VIII's bull *Unam sanctam* of 1302 which not only claimed that 'it is altogether necessary to salvation for every human creature to be subject to the Roman Pontiff', but also insisted that the pope's spiritual power was divine rather than human and that 'if the supreme spiritual power errs it can be judged only by God not by man'.

[209] The great twelfth-century canonist, Gratian of Bologna, who was largely responsible for systematising canon law in his *Concordia Discordantium Canonum* ('Concord of Discordant Canons'), generally insisted that the pope was immune from human judgement, but did provide a loophole in the phrase 'unless he is found straying from the faith'. Subsequent canonists were to exploit this, albeit with great caution, and extend it to include not just a heretical pope but one who threatened the welfare of the Christian community.

[210] Buchanan has already alluded in general terms to the distinction between the office and the person of a magistrate, but now he focuses attention on the principle, deeply rooted in medieval theology and canon law, that the pope can be distinguished from the papal office. Originally, as Buchanan suggests, this distinction was developed to protect the infallibility of the 'vicar of Christ', but it also proved the

means by which conciliar theorists were able to justify the deposition of an individual pope without impugning the integrity of the papacy as such.

[211] The early history of the papacy, particularly from the seventh to the eleventh centuries, when the bishops of Rome were often imperial puppets or victims of the vicious feuding of the Roman aristocracy, is littered with examples of abdications, depositions and assassinations. But Buchanan clearly has in mind Pope Formosus (891-96) who was exhumed by his successor, Stephen VI, enthroned in full pontifical dress, and subjected to a mock trial; on being found guilty, his body was first left in a common grave and then dumped in the Tiber. Stephen was in his turn deposed and subsequently strangled. Later in the *Dialogue*, Buchanan makes more explicit reference both to the Council of Constance (1414-18), which deposed two popes or anti-popes (John XXIII and Benedict XIII), forced the resignation of a third (Gregory XII) and elected Martin V in their place, and to the attempts of the Council of Basle (1431-49) to secure the deposition of Eugenius IV.

[212] Buchanan had good reason to dislike Gian Petro Carafa (1476-1559), Pope Paul IV (1555-59), who as a militant Catholic reformer was associated with the creation of both the Inquisition and the papal Index of Prohibited Books. On the eve of his death in 1559 a mob mutilated the pope's statue and set fire to the prisons of the Roman Inquisition, freeing the prisoners. Following his death, by a decree of the Roman people, his family's coat-of-arms and inscriptions were defaced and removed.

[213] No patristic or sixteenth-century source has been identified for Buchanan's breakdown of the Christian communities that Paul was addressing and it seems likely that his remarks are based on such fleeting references to the names and status of its members as occur in Acts and in the greetings-lists of the Pauline Epistles themselves (e.g., Romans, i, 1-15; I Corinthians, xvi, 10-19).

[214] Buchanan evidently has in mind here, and again in the next paragraph, not so much Paul's Epistle to the Romans, as his strictures on personal morality and social order in I Corinthians, vii, and perhaps particularly Ephesians, v, and vi, 1-9, and Colossians, iii, 18-22.

[215] Jeremiah, xxvii. What follows in this paragraph reflects both on Paul's instruction to obey the otherwise unspecified 'higher powers' in Romans, xiii, and on the more specific familial and social obligations as set out by Paul in the Epistles.

[216] Luke, xviii, 2.

[217] In addition to the texts already cited, Buchanan presumably has in mind I Corinthians, v, 11 (to which he refers again below).

[218] An assumption that was by no means confined to 'servile courtiers': Calvin makes the point in his *Institutes*, IV, xx, 25. Marian exiles such as Knox and Goodman also viewed Mary Tudor's persecution of English Protestants as God's punishment of a sinful people.

[219] Cf. Calvin, *Institutes*, IV, xx, 30. In 1554, John Knox, as yet unwilling or unable to justify organised resistance to Mary Tudor's Catholic regime, famously prayed that God stir up some Phinehas, Elijah or Jehu to suppress idolatry in England. However, none of these Old Testament heroes could be described as 'humble and obscure'.

[220] Buchanan ends this section as he began it with what amounts to an attack on the tyranny of custom. In the *History* (II, pp. 306, 502; XIV, xliii, XVIII, xxv), he comments that the laws of Scotland consist essentially of parliamentary statutes and that these are generally temporary rather than fixed.

221 Buchanan finally concludes his discussion of scriptural arguments for unstinting obedience by emphasising that the history of the Jewish people, precisely because of the Jews' unique relationship with God, is a special case with no universal validity. In Buchanan's view, therefore, the Bible does not conflict with the principle, to which he now returns, that it is permissible for the people to hold their rulers to account. The final section of the *Dialogue* is devoted to exploring, first, the equity of this principle, and second, its practicality, culminating in a ringing endorsement of the legitimacy of single-handed tyrannicide.

222 Publius Cornelius Lentulus Sura, praetor for the second time in 63 BC, was one of Catiline's most prominent supporters in the anti-republican conspiracy of that year. Following his arrest, he was forced to resign his praetorship and was subsequently executed by strangulation. Sallust, *Catiline*, lv, 1-6; Cicero, *In Catilinam*, iii, 14-15.

223 According to Roman tradition, a board of ten patricians was given power in 451 BC to prepare a code of laws (the Twelve Tables). They began this task but were succeeded by a second board of *decemvirs* who, despite being partly plebeian, were thought to have behaved tyrannically and were eventually forced out of office (Livy, III, xxx-liv).

224 Buchanan has already referred to Chilperic (Childeric III). There are several examples from the early history of Venice of doges abdicating, either voluntarily or under compulsion, and two of the great doges of the twelfth century, Domenico Michiel (d. 1130) and Sebastiano Ziani (d. 1178), retired to the monastery of San Giorgio Maggiore.

225 Christian or Christiern II (1481-1549) was king of Denmark-Norway (1513-23) and of Sweden (1520-23). However, his military conquest of Sweden and bloody repression of opposition in the so-called 'Stockholm bloodbath' led to a major revolt which saw Gustavus I Vasa appointed king in his place. Christian's failure in

Sweden immediately precipitated a further revolt in Denmark which forced him off the throne in favour of his uncle, Frederick. A failed attempt in 1531 to regain his kingdom ended in his arrest the following year and he spent the remainder of his life in various Danish prisons.

[226] Normally at Rome a dictator was appointed by the consuls to deal with a short-term emergency, but Buchanan may be thinking here of Livy's account (XXII, viii) of how, after the Roman defeat at Trasimene in 217 BC, Fabius Maximus was chosen dictator 'by popular election'.

[227] Buchanan is evidently thinking of Roman law which subjected a freedman after his emancipation to various penalties if he was found to be 'ungrateful' and in breach of his obligations to his former master; see, e.g., *Digest*, XXV, iii, 6 (1), and XXXVII, xiv, 5.

[228] A reference primarily to the early kings of Scots, many of whom were held to account by their subjects, whose reigns were chronicled in Hector Boece's *Scotorum Historia*.

[229] On Culen and Evenus, see above pp. 176-7. Buchanan might have in mind either Ferchard I, fifty-second king of Scots, or Ferchard II, fifty-fourth king of Scots. Hector Boece gives a lengthy account of the vicious tyranny of Ferchard I, including his falling into Pelagian heresy, his seizure and imprisonment by the nobility, and his subsequent suicide (*Scotorum Historia*, fo. clxxix[r-v]). His account of Ferchard II's reign is hardly less elaborate: as lecherous as he was avaricious, he murdered his wife and raped his daughters and was only saved from execution at the hands of the nobility by suffering a wolf bite that infected his whole body and caused him such distress that he was eventually brought publicly to repent his sins and seek absolution from St Colman (*ibid.*, fo. clxxxiii[r-v]). In keeping with his usual practice, in his own *History*, Buchanan drastically shortens Boece's versions, retaining their substance but, in the process, highlighting the role of the nobility in calling such tyrants to account (*History*, I, pp. 252, 254; V, xxxix).

[230] Buchanan has already mentioned in passing the death of James III at or after the battle of Sauchieburn near Stirling on 11 June 1488. Despite the late king's deep unpopularity, however, and the presence in their ranks of his fifteen year-old son, crowned James IV at Scone on 24 June, the victorious rebels were initially reluctant to expose their actions to scrutiny and delayed summoning a meeting of the Three Estates until 6 October. When Parliament did finally meet, the attendance was unusually large, and the rebel lords had considerable difficulty in controlling it. Unable to prevent a full-scale debate, they defended themselves by producing a copy of an agreement signed by James III in April 1488 on which he had promptly reneged. This was incorporated into a parliamentary statute that became the official justification of the proceedings against James III, and on which Buchanan is drawing here. Buchanan will have known the details of the act through the 1566 edition of the *Actis and Constitutionis*, fos. lxxxii^v-lxxxiii^r (cf. *APS*, II, pp. 210-11, c. 5).

[231] Buchanan is drawing here on Livy, IV, xii-xvi, where he describes how in 439 BC Gaius Servilius Ahala, master of horse to Lucius Quinctius (the dictator Cincinnatus), thwarted the ambition of Spurius Maelius to make himself king by confronting him in the Forum and killing him as he fled (literally turning his back). Cincinnatus then defended Ahala's action in a colourful anti-monarchical speech that deplored the attempt to enslave and tyrannise over the Roman people.

[232] By implication, according to Buchanan, the act that exonerated the rebels of 1488, and in effect justified their resistance to James III's tyrannical regime, lent constitutional legitimacy to the actions of those who had overthrown Mary in 1567.

[233] Cf. the opening pages of the *Dialogue*, where Maitland, newly returned from France, reports on the sense of outrage there at what had occurred in Scotland.

[234] In the original Latin text, Buchanan's use of the Greek term *paranomias* ('unconstitutionality') perhaps suggests that he is thinking of ancient Athens where the mover of any law or decree could be indicted under a *graphe paranomon* if his proposal was shown to be contrary to existing law or the public interest.

[235] Buchanan is contrasting Roman and Scottish practice: twenty-four days was the usual interval between the promulgation of a bill at Rome and the meeting of the assembly to vote on it (see, e.g., Livy, III, xxxv, 1); in Scotland, meetings of Parliament were held at forty days notice.

[236] Cf. the dedication to James VI above pp. 37-8, where Buchanan describes flattery as 'the nurse of tyranny and the most grievous plague of lawful kingship'.

[237] Cf. Plato, *Republic*, 588-9, where 'ancient stories' of fabulous monsters made up of several creatures are recalled in order to illustrate the 'civil war' in the human soul and the need to subject man's animal passions to the rule of reason. More generally, what follows in the next paragraph is clearly indebted to the discussion in Book IX of the *Republic* of the tyrannical man whose appetites overwhelm reason and who is prey to the beast within the soul.

[238] See, e. g., Horace, *Odes*, I, xvi, 13-16: 'Prometheus, as goes the tale, when forced to add to our primeval clay a portion drawn from every creature, put also in our breasts the fury of the ravening lion'.

[239] See Aristotle, *Politics*, III, xvi, 5 (1287a).

[240] No obvious source for this comparison has been identified, though Plato, *Statesman*, 290b, may have influenced it.

[241] In the interchange that follows Buchanan is at his most Platonic in his mode of argument. The simile pursued, however, was probably

suggested by the opening paragraph of Aristotle's *Ethics*, I, i (1094a).

[242] Buchanan's reference to the role of Roman tribunes and Spartan ephors in restraining a tyrant is strongly reminiscent of the highly influential passage to the same effect in Calvin, *Institutes*, IV, xx, 31 (discussed above).

[243] Maitland perhaps has in mind the account in Herodotus, III, 83-88, of how Darius was chosen king of Persia, not so much by arbitration, as by a (rigged) horserace between the six competitors for the throne.

[244] Buchanan eschews the obvious example of the succession being settled by arbitration – Edward I's adjudication in the 'Great Cause' in 1292 – in favour of a much more obscure episode which was alleged to have followed Kenneth III's attempt to change the succession laws in favour of male primogeniture. According to his account in the *History* (I, pp. 314-16; VI, xlv-xlvii), the claim to the throne of Kenneth's son, Malcolm II (Mael Coluim mac Cinaeda), was challenged by Grim (Giric) who also had himself declared king. To avoid armed conflict, Bishop Fothadus arranged a settlement whereby 'Grim should retain the title of king so long as he lived; that on his death the kingdom should revert to Malcolm, and, that afterward the law of Kenneth, establishing the succession to the kingdom in the children of the king, should be sacred and inviolable'. What Buchanan fails to mention in the *Dialogue* is that the arbitration failed and that the dispute was finally settled in Malcolm's favour through trial of battle. Bower, *Scotichronicon*, II, pp. 383-5, 395-7, notes the disputed succession and that the outcome was decided by battle, but makes no mention of arbitration. Once again, however, the story as told by Buchanan is an abbreviated version of the account in Boece, *Scotorum Historia*, fo. ccxliv[r-v].

[245] In Rome, 'veto' was the word used by tribunes of the people to object to a proposal made by the senate or a magistrate. However,

Maitland's point here, which Buchanan will dispute, is that the king has in effect the power to veto the decisions of any judges before whom he appears.

246 In his reference to the 'greater part' (*maior pars*), Buchanan is using a technical term in medieval canon law, applied to the election of the pope by the college of cardinals as well as that of bishops by their chapters. While it might mean a simple numerical majority, from an early date a degree of ambiguity was introduced by adding a qualitative dimension to an otherwise simple arithmetical calculation. Thus, often with reference to Aristotle's discussion of the need to balance quantity and quality in constitutional arrangements (*Politics*, IV, xii, 1-2 (1296b)), the majority came to be defined in such formulae as the 'greater and more reasonable part' (*maior et sanior pars*). Frequently invoked by fifteenth-century conciliar theorists in the context of voting in church councils, it was not normally applied, as it is here, to the people as a whole. However, just as Buchanan leaves unclear to whom or what the people – or the majority of them – transfer their sovereign authority, so the following discussion of citizenship ends up echoing the more ambiguous formulations of the canonists and conciliarists.

247 Juvenal, *Satires*, XIII, 26-27.

248 See Ovid, *Ex Ponto*, II, iii, 7-10, where he reflects on how few had stood by him at the time of his banishment from Rome.

249 Buchanan's 'not only the better part but also the greater' (*pars melior sed etiam maior*) is reminiscent of the formula *maior et sanior pars* referred to above.

250 That is, minor property disputes; for a similar formulation, see Cicero, *De Oratore*, I, xxxviii, 173.

251 The saying was all but proverbial in the sixteenth century, but see Plutarch, *Solon*, v, 2, where Anacharsis is said to have laughed at

Solon 'for thinking that he could check the injustice and rapacity of the citizens by written laws, which were just like spiders' webs; they would hold the weak and delicate who might be caught in their meshes, but would be torn in pieces by the rich and powerful'.

[252] See Psalm lxxxii, 6. James VI would rest his claim to rule by divine right on the same scriptural authority; see *True Lawe of Free Monarchies*, in *Minor Prose Works*, p. 61.

[253] In this further dig at papal pretensions, Buchanan presumably has in mind such examples as Gregory VII's claim in his *Dictatus Papae* of 1075 that 'the pope is the only one whose feet are to be kissed by all princes'. Gregory subsequently forced the Emperor Henry IV into a humiliating submission to his authority in 1077 at Canossa in northern Italy. Exactly a century later, in 1177, Frederick Barbarossa suffered similar humiliation at the hands of Pope Alexander III, being obliged to attend on him in Venice and hold his stirrup while the pope mounted his horse. More generally, however, Buchanan is simply echoing much sixteenth-century anti-papal polemic.

[254] Pope John XXII (1316-34) was declared deposed by the German king, Louis IV, in 1328, and in the last years of his pontificate was condemned as a heretic before repenting on his deathbed. However, it is the antipope John XXIII (1410-15) to whom Buchanan is referring here. His flight and capture during the early stages of the Council of Constance culminated in his deposition and imprisonment. Held in captivity until 1419, when he secured his release through payment of a hefty ransom, he then formally submitted to Martin V whose election at Constance in 1417 had finally brought the Great Schism to an end.

[255] The acts and decrees of the Council of Basle (1431-49) were first published in 1499 and frequently reissued in the sixteenth century. From the outset of this long-running synod, the authority of a general council of the church over the pope, first asserted in the decree

Sacrosancta (1415) of the Council of Constance, was re-affirmed. However, Pope Eugenius IV refused to recognise the Basle assembly and, although his attempts to dissolve it failed, he ignored the council's 1436 summons to stand trial for disobeying its decrees. Instead he transferred the council to Ferrara, where negotiations with the Greek Church over resolving the ancient schism between it and Rome were on-going, and where many of the higher ranking clerics from Basle decided to join him. Those who remained at Basle proceeded to suspend and then in 1439 to depose Eugenius and elect Felix V in his place. The resulting schism lasted ten years until, in 1449, the anti-pope Felix was forced to resign and the Council of Basle, before dissolving itself, duly recognised the reigning pope, Nicholas V, who had succeeded Eugenius IV on his death in 1447. Although this outcome suggests that papal authority was ultimately victorious, it was a victory achieved at the expense of major concessions to secular powers, such as the French king and the German emperor, eager to assert greater authority over ecclesiastical revenues and appointments. At the same time the schism saw the consolidation and elaboration of the kind of conciliarist ideas that Buchanan's teacher, John Mair, was to help re-state and popularise in the early sixteenth century.

[256] Buchanan's gloss on the events to which he has been alluding is perhaps ironic and is certainly unconvincing. In fact, not only did the ecclesiastical schisms of the late fourteenth and fifteenth centuries make clear that kings were unwilling to acknowledge the superior majesty of popes, but on no occasion did a pope willingly suffer the indignity of having his authority impugned and undermined by a council, let alone the still greater indignity of personally pleading his cause before such a body.

[257] Titius, Sempronius and Stichus are used as stock names in fictitious cases throughout the *Digest*.

[258] Buchanan rather surprisingly blunts the effectiveness of this reference to the famous *Digna vox* edict of 429 (*Codex*, I, xiv, 4), issued by the joint Emperors Theodosius and Valentinian, by omitting both a crucial clause from the first sentence and a crucial pronoun from the last. As well as dropping the emperors' highly pertinent admission that 'our authority depends on the authority of the law', Buchanan lessens the force of the final sentence, which might be translated: 'And by the present solemn edict we declare to others what we do not allow as lawful to ourselves.'

[259] For the emperor's participation in such contests, see Suetonius, *Nero*, xxiii-xxiv.

[260] Leviticus, xix, 15.

[261] Lucan, *Civil War*, V, 298-90.

[262] See Buchanan's earlier reference to Hiero, tyrant of Syracuse.

[263] The opportunity presents itself here for Buchanan to argue that it is only once the ruler has been judged to be tyrannical by some such formal body as a court, council or parliament that he may be legitimately resisted. This he does not do, however, preferring instead to pursue in what follows the far more radical line that a ruler who breaks the terms of the 'pact' or 'contract' with his people effectively stands self-condemned as a public enemy whom the community or even individual citizens may lawfully kill.

[264] This distinction in Roman law goes back to the Twelve Tables (see *Digest*, XLVII, 55(2)), but Buchanan's wording here is closer to Cicero, *Pro Milone*, iii, 9.

[265] See the reference above to Thebe, Timoleon and Cassius. Sallust, *Catiline*, xxxix, 5, does not allow us to identify Fulvius precisely, simply referring to him as a senator's son. The Brutus Buchanan has

in mind here is not Marcus Junius Brutus, famed for the assassination of Julius Caesar in 44 BC, but Lucius Junius Brutus, renowned for having freed Rome from tyranny, who as consul subsequently presided over the execution of his own two sons as well as other noble youths for conspiring to restore the Tarquins to power (see Livy, II, v, 5-9).

[266] Cults honouring tyrannicides were not uncommon in ancient Greece, but Buchanan is drawing here on *De Officiis*, III, iv, 19, and particularly III, iv, 32, where Cicero argues that 'we have no ties of fellowship with a tyrant ... all that pestilent and abominable race should be exterminated from human society'.

[267] Domitius Corbulo, Nero's most notable general, commanded his forces in various eastern campaigns. Dio Cassius (*Roman History*, LXII, vi, 4) recounts how, when in 66 AD he brought Tiradates to Rome to receive the crown of Armenia from Nero in person, Tiradates 'praised Corbulo, in whom he found only one fault, that he would put up with such a master'.

[268] See Dio Cassius, *Roman History*, LIX, xxx, 2.

[269] That is, the deposition and imprisonment of Mary Stewart.

[270] The latter part of this sentence reshapes Livy, III, liv, 3, while the former alludes to the sword which the tyrant Dionysius left hanging by a horse thread over the neck of the flatterer Damocles to illustrate how little he was able to enjoy the riches that surrounded him; see Cicero, *Tusculan Disputations*, V, xxi, 61-2.

[271] Vespasian became Roman emperor amid the violence of 69 AD, but according to Tacitus, *Histories*, I, 50, 'unlike all his predecessors, he was the only emperor who was changed for the better by his office'. His elder son, Titus, who succeeded him in 79 and reigned for only two years, was alleged to have poisoned him, but the story is rejected

by Dio Cassius who observed that Titus 'ruled with mildness and died at the height of his glory', though adding that his high reputation was the result of the brevity of his reign (*Roman History*, LXVI, xvii, 1; LXVI, xviii, 5). That of Pertinax was even briefer – he reigned for three months in 193 – and, though believed to have been party to the conspiracy which removed his detested predecessor, Commodus, he gained popularity for the reforms he instituted (Dio Cassius, *Roman History*, LXXIV, i-x). Alexander III (the Great) succeeded to the throne of Macedon after the assassination of his father Philip in 336 BC and against a background of bloody dynastic intrigue (Diodorus, XVII, ii ff). Elsewhere, in contrast to many contemporaries, Buchanan is less than complimentary about his subsequent imperial exploits, describing him as 'the world's most famous robber,/ Living for the destruction of the globe,/ Dying in dishonour' (*Political Poetry*, pp. 84-5). Both Hiero I and Hiero II seized power in Syracuse by violence, but thereafter ruled moderately, gaining popular respect and approval.

[272] I Corinthians, v, 11.

[273] After the Emperor Theodosius had caused the massacre of several thousand of the inhabitants of Thessalonica in 390, Ambrose, Bishop of Milan, insisted on his public repentance before re-admitting him to the church.

[274] Buchanan is referring to a Roman formula for outlawry (see Cicero, *Phillipics*, I, ix, 23), here paralleling the ultimate ecclesiastical sanction of excommunication.

[275] A reference to the alleged foundation of the Scottish kingdom by the legendary Fergus I in 330 BC.

[276] An unlikely gloss on recent Scottish history, but perhaps Buchanan has in mind Mary's surrender to the Confederate Lords at Carberry Hill on 15 June 1567. Although hardly free of altercation –

Bothwell proposed settling the affair through single combat with a confederate champion – no blood was spilt and Mary was taken first to Edinburgh and then to Lochleven where she was forced to abdicate in her son's favour on 24 July.

277 Seneca, *Thyestes*, 344-390.

Bibliography

Buchanan's writings

Opera Omnia, ed. T. Ruddiman (Edinburgh, 1715).

The Political Poetry, ed. and trans. P. J. McGinnis and A. H. Williamson (Scottish History Society, 1995).

History of Scotland, ed. and trans. J.Aikman (Glasgow, 1827).

The Tragedies, ed. and trans. P. Sharratt and P.G. Walsh (Edinburgh, 1983).

The Tyrannous Reign of Mary Queen of Scots: George Buchanan's Account, ed. and trans. W.A. Gatherer (Edinburgh, 1958).

A Dialogue on the Law of Kingship among the Scots; A Critical Edition and Translation of George Buchanan's 'De Iure Regni apud Scotos Dialogus', ed. and trans. R. A. Mason and M. S. Smith (Aldershot, 2004).

Sources referred to in the notes

The Actis and Constitutionis of the Realme of Scotland (Edinburgh, 1566).

Acts of the Parliaments of Scotland, ed. T. Thomson and C. Innes (Edinburgh, 1814-75).

Aitken, J. M. (ed.), *The Trial of George Buchanan Before the Lisbon Inquisition* (Edinburgh, 1939).

Aristotle, *The Politics of Aristotle*, ed. and trans. Ernest Barker (Oxford, 1946).

Aristotle, *Nichomachean Ethics*, ed. and trans. David Ross (World's Classics edn., London, 1954).

Aristotle, *The 'Art' of Rhetoric*, ed. and trans. J.H. Freese (Loeb edn., 1926).

Barclay, William, *De Regno et Regali Potestate Adversus Buchananum, Brutum, Boucherium & Reliquos Monarchomachos* (Paris, 1600).

Boece, Hector, *Scotorum Historiae a Prima Gentis Origine* (Paris, 1527).

Bower, Walter, *Scotichronicon*, ed. D. E. R. Watt (Aberdeen and Edinburgh, 1987-98).

Calvin, John, *Institutes of the Christian Religion*, ed. and trans. Henry Beveridge (London, 1949).

Calvin, John, *Commentary on the Epistle of St Paul to the Romans*, ed. and trans. John Owen, Calvin Translation Society (Edinburgh, 1849).

Chrysostom, St John, *Homilies on the Acts of the Apostles and the Epistle to the Romans*, Library of the Nicene and Post-Nicene Fathers XI (Grand Rapids, Mich., 1997).

Cicero, *Brutus*, ed. and trans. G. L. Hendrickson (Loeb edn., 1939).

Cicero, *De Inventione*, ed. and trans. H. M. Hubbell (Loeb edn., 1949).

Cicero, De *Natura Deorum*, ed. and trans. H. Rackham (Loeb edn., 1933).

Cicero, *De Officiis*, ed. and trans. W. Miller (Loeb edn., 1913).

Cicero, *De Oratore*, ed. and trans. E. W. Sutton and H. Rackham (Loeb edn., 1942-48).

Cicero, *De Re Publica and De Legibus*, ed. and trans. C. W. Keyes (Loeb edn., 1928).

Cicero, *Letters to Atticus*, ed. and trans. E. O. Winstedt (Loeb edn., 1912-18).

Cicero, *Letters to His Brother Quintus*, ed. and trans. W. G. Williams (Loeb edn., 1989).

Cicero, *Philippics*, ed. and trans. D. R. Shackleton Bailey (Chapel Hill and London, 1986).

Cicero, *The Speeches* [*Pro Milone*], ed. and trans. N. H. Watts (Loeb edn., 1931).

Cicero, *Tusculan Disputations*, ed. and trans. J. E. King (Loeb edn., 1927).

Cicero, *The Verrine Orations*, ed. and trans. L. H. G. Greenwood (Loeb edn., 1928-35).

Claudian, ed. and trans. M. Platnauer (Loeb edn., 1922).

Curtius, *History of Alexander*, ed. and trans. J. C. Rolfe (Loeb edn., 1946).

Decrees of the Ecumenical Councils, ed. N. P. Tanner (London and Washington, DC, 1990).

Demosthenes, *On the Crown*, ed. and trans. S. Usher (Warminster, 1993).

Dio Cassius, *Roman History*, ed. and trans. E. Cary (Loeb edn., 1914-27).

Diodorus of Sicily, ed. and trans. C. H. Oldfather et al. (Loeb edn., 1933-67).

Dionysius of Halicarnassus, *The Roman Antiquities*, ed. and trans. E. Cary (Loeb edn., 1937-50).

Erasmus, Desiderius, *Adages*, in *Collected Works of Erasmus*, vols. 30-34 (Toronto, Buffalo and London, 1982-92).

Erasmus, Desiderius, *The Education of a Christian Prince*, in *Collected Works of Erasmus*, vols. 27-28 (Toronto, Buffalo and London, 1986).

Herodotus, *The Histories*, trans. R. Waterfield with an introduction and notes by C. Dewald (Oxford, 1998).

Homer, *The Iliad*, ed. and trans. E. V. Rieu (Penguin Classics edn., Harmondsworth, 1950).

Homer, *The Odyssey*, ed. and trans. E.V. Rieu (Penguin Classics edn., Harmondsworth, 1945).

Horace, *Odes and Epodes*, ed. and trans. C. E. Bennet (Loeb edn., 1988).

Horace, Satires, *Epistles and Ars Poetica*, ed. and trans. H. Rushton Fairclough (Loeb edn., 1926).

James VI and I, *Minor Prose Works*, ed. J. Craigie (Scottish Text Society, 1982).

Justinian, *The Digest of Justinian*, ed. and trans. T. Mommsen, P. Krueger and A. Watson (Philadelphia, 1985).

Justinian, *The Institutes*, ed. and trans. P. Birks and G. McLeod (London, 1987).

Juvenal, *Juvenal and Persius*, ed. and trans. G. G. Ramsay (Loeb edn., 1940).

Livy, *Ab Urbe Condita*, ed. and trans. B. O. Foster *et al*. (Loeb edn., 1919-59).

Lucan, *The Civil War*, ed. and trans. J. D. Duff (Loeb edn., 1928).

Mair, John, *A History of Greater Britain as well England as Scotland*, ed. and trans. A. Constable (Scottish History Society, 1892).

Ovid, *Metamorphoses*, ed. and trans. F. J. Miller (Loeb edn., 1916).

Ovid, *Tristia. Ex Ponto*, ed. and trans. A. L. Wheeler (Loeb edn., 1924).

Pausanias, *Description of Greece*, ed. and trans. W. H. S. Jones *et al*. (Loeb edn., 1918-25).

Persius, *The Satires*, ed. and trans. J. R. Jenkinson (Warminster, 1980).

Petronius, ed. and trans. M. Heseltine (Loeb edn., 1913).

Plato, *The Dialogues of Plato*, ed. and trans. B. Jowett (4th edn., Oxford, 1953).

Plato, *Epistles*, ed. and trans. J. B. Bury (Loeb edn., 1942).

Plautus, ed. and trans. P. Nixon (Loeb edn., 1916).

Pliny, *Natural History*, ed. and trans. H. Rackham *et al*. (Loeb edn., 1938-62).

Plutarch, *Lives*, ed. and trans. B. Perrin (Loeb edn., 1914-26).

Plutarch, *Moralia*, ed. and trans. F. C. Babbit *et al*. (Loeb edn., 1927-69).

Polybius, *Histories*, ed. and trans. W. R. Paton (Loeb edn., 1922-27).

Quintilian, *Institutio Oratoria*, ed. and trans. H. E. Butler (Loeb edn., 1921-22).

Sallust, ed. and trans. J. C. Rolfe (Loeb edn., 1921).

Seneca, *Moral Essays*, ed. and trans. J. W. Basore (Loeb edn., 1928-35).

Strabo, *The Geography of Strabo*, ed. and trans. H. L. Jones (Loeb edn., 1917-32).

Suetonius, *Lives of the Caesars and Lives of Illustrious Men*, ed. and trans. J. C. Rolfe (Loeb edn., 1914).

Terence, ed. and trans. J. Sargeaunt (Loeb edn., 1912).

Tacitus, *Annals*, ed. and trans. J. Jackson (Loeb edn., 1931-37).

Virgil, *Eclogues, Georgics and Aeneid*, ed. and trans. H. Rushton Fairclough (Loeb edn., 1934-35).

Xenophon, *Scripta Minora* [*Hiero, Agesilaus and Spartan Constitution*], ed. and trans. E. C. Marchant (Loeb edn., 1925).

Works on Buchanan

Bonner, E., 'French Naturalisation of the Scots in the Fifteenth and Sixteenth Centuries', *Historical Journal*, 40 (1997), pp. 1085-1115.

Burns, J. H., *The True Law of Kingship: Concepts of Monarchy in Early Modern Scotland* (Oxford, 1996).

Burns, J. H. (ed.), *The Cambridge History of Political Thought, 1450-1700* (Cambridge, 1991).

Davidson, P., Montserrat, D. and Stevenson, J., 'Three Entertainments for the Wedding of Mary Queen of Scots Written by George Buchanan: Latin Text and Translation', *Scotlands*, 2 (1995), pp. 1-10.

Duncan, D., *Thomas Ruddiman: A Study in Scottish Scholarship of the Early Eighteenth Century* (Edinburgh, 1965).

Durkan, J. (ed.), *A Bibliography of George Buchanan* (Glasgow, 1994).

Hume Brown, P., *George Buchanan: Humanist and Reformer* (Edinburgh, 1890).

Lynch, M., 'Queen Mary's Triumph: The Baptismal Celebrations at Stirling in December 1566', *Scottish Historical Review*, 69 (1990), pp. 1-21.

McFarlane, I. D., *Buchanan* (London, 1981).

McKechnie, W. S., 'Thomas Maitland', *Scottish Historical Review*, 4 (1906-7), pp. 274-93.

Mason, R. A., *Kingship and the Commonweal: Political Thought in Renaissance and Reformation Scotland* (East Linton, 1998).

Mason, R. A., 'George Buchanan and Mary Queen of Scots', *Records of the Scottish Church History Society*, 30 (2000), pp. 1-27.

Mason, R. A., 'Civil Society and the Celts: Hector Boece, George Buchanan and the Ancient Scottish Past', in E. J. Cowan and R. J. Finlay (eds.), *Scottish History: The Power of the Past* (Edinburgh, 2002), pp. 95-119.

Phillips, J. E., 'George Buchanan and the Sidney Circle', *Huntington Library Quarterly*, 12 (1948-49), pp. 23-55.

Salmon, J. H. M., 'An Alternative Theory of Popular Resistance: Buchanan, Rossaeus and Locke', in J. H. M. Salmon, *Renaissance and Revolt: Essays in the Intellectual and Social History of Early Modern France* (Cambridge, 1987), pp. 136-54.

Skinner, Q., *The Foundations of Modern Political Thought* (Cambridge, 1978).

Trevor-Roper, H. R., 'George Buchanan and the Ancient Scottish Constitution', *English Historical Review*, Supplement 3 (1966).

Williamson, A. H., *Scottish National Consciousness in the Age of James VI* (Edinburgh, 1979).

Wormald, Jenny, *Mary Queen of Scots: A Study in Failure* (London, 1988).

Index

Aeneas 52, 153
Aeschylus 167
Ahab 116, 185
Ahala, Gaius Servilius 123, 191
Agamemnon 51, 153
Agesilaus, king of Sparta 61, 156, 157
Alcibiades 43, 149
Alexander the Great 144, 167, 199
Alexander, tyrant of Pherae 97-8, 172
Alexander III, king of Scots 16, 180
Althusius, Johannes 23
Ambrose 145, 199
Appian 174
Appius Claudius 76, 161
Arbuthnett, Alexander 18
Aristophanes 167
Aristotle 11, 62, 69, 93, 126, 149, 151, 152-4, 155, 157, 158, 160, 161, 167, 168, 179, 182, 192, 193, 194
Augustus, Roman emperor 163, 164, 168

Balliol, John 106, 180
Barclay, William 22
Beale, Robert 33
Beaton, Cardinal David 3
Belisarius 100, 174
Bellerophon of Corinth 48
Beza, Theodore 9, 185
Boece, Hector 15, 175, 176, 177, 190, 193
Boniface VIII, pope 161, 186
Bothwell, James Hepburn, Earl of 6, 7, 200
Bower, Walter 175, 176, 177
Brissac, marèchal de 4

Brown, Peter Hume 27
Brutus, Lucius Junius 198
Brutus, Marcus Junius 141-2, 198

Caligula, Roman emperor 44, 78-9, 98-9, 111, 113, 142, 150, 183
Calvin, John 179, 182, 184, 185, 188, 193
Catiline 122, 141, 189, 197
Charles I, king of Great Britain 22, 23
Charles II, king of Great Britain 23-24
Charles V, Holy Roman Emperor 181
Childeric III, see Chilperic
Chilperic 77, 122, 161-2, 189
Christian, king of Denmark 122, 189-90
Chrysostom 112, 183, 184, 185
Cicero 10-11, 17, 49, 61-2, 74, 150-1, 152, 154, 155, 157, 158, 159, 160, 161, 165, 166, 167, 168, 170, 172, 174, 177-8, 189, 194, 197, 198, 199
Cincinnatus (Lucius Quinctius), 123, 155, 191
Claudian 85, 165
Claudius, Roman emperor 111, 183
Cleomenes, king of Sparta 61
Cosimo di Medici 93, 170
Cromwell, Oliver 23
Culen, king of Scots 101, 122, 176, 190
Cyrus the Great 157

Darius, king of Persia 193
Darnley, Henry Stewart, Lord 5-6, 149
David, king of Israel 106, 155, 181

Dio Cassius 163, 173, 198-9
Dionysius, tyrant of Syracuse 97, 172
Dionysius of Halicarnassus 151, 161, 168, 172
Domitian, Roman emperor 44, 113, 150, 175
Domitius Corbulo 142, 198

Edward I, king of England 106, 180, 193
Elijah 188
Elizabeth Tudor 7, 18
Erasmus 2, 10, 166, 170-1, 183
Eugenius IV, pope 196
Euripides 3, 166
Evenus, king of Scots 101, 122, 177, 190

Ferchard I, king of Scots 123, 190
Ferchard II, king of Scots 190
Ferdinand of Aragon 77, 162
Fergus I, king of Scots 199
Ferguson, Adam 25
Fletcher, Andrew, of Saltoun 25

Galen 152
Goodman, Christopher 9, 188
Gratian 186
Gregory VII, pope 161, 195
Grim, king of Scots 130, 193
Grotius, Hugo 23

Helen of Troy 89-90, 166
Henry of Luxembourg 77, 162
Herodotus 62, 110, 156, 157, 182, 193
Hiero, tyrant of Syracuse 93, 144, 157, 170, 197, 199

Homer 47, 150, 151, 153
Horace 89, 150, 152, 158, 166, 174, 192
Hume, David, of Godscroft 21-22

Innocent III, pope 161, 162

James I, king of Scots 101, 175
James III, king of Scots 16, 101, 123, 176, 191
James IV, king of Scots 101, 176, 191
James V, king of Scots, 3, 6
James VI, king of Scots, 1, 5, 8, 20-21, 22, 37-8, 154, 160, 171, 180, 182, 192, 195
James VII and II, king of Great Britain 24
Jehu 188
Jeremiah 115, 120
Jerome 184
John, king of Navarre 77
John XXII, pope 134, 195
John XXIII, pope 134, 187, 195
Judas Iscariot 91, 168
Julius Caesar 168, 169
Julius III, pope 79, 163
Justinian 100, 174
Juvenal 151, 152, 156, 175, 194

Kenneth III (II), king of Scots 14, 16, 101-2, 177, 178, 193
Knox, John 5, 9-10, 26, 188

Leicester, Robert Dudley, Earl of 21
Leonidas, king of Sparta 61, 156, 157
Livy 153, 154, 155, 156, 158, 161, 166, 171, 172, 173, 178, 189, 190, 191, 192, 198
Locke, John 11, 25

Lucan 139, 197
Lucius Quinctius, see *Cincinnatus*
Luther, Martin, 2
Lycurgus 156

McFarlan, Robert 26
Mair (Major), John, 2, 11, 175, 180, 196
Maitland, Thomas 10, 29, 149
Malcolm II, king of Scots 130, 193
Mary, Queen of Scots, 1, 4-8, 15, 17, 19, 149, 181, 191, 198, 199-200
Mary Tudor 188
Melville, Andrew 18, 21-22
Milton, John 23, 24
Mithridates, king of Pontus 160, 173
Moray, James Stewart, Earl of 6-8, 17
Moses 66, 87, 157

Nebuchadnezzar, king of Babylon 185
Nero, Roman emperor 44, 91, 111, 113, 135, 142, 150, 168, 183, 198
Numa Pompilius 86, 166

Ovid 152, 168, 194

Paul, St 9-10, 69, 111-121, 144-5, 158, 183, 184, 185, 186, 187, 188
Paul IV, pope 117, 187
Pelagius (Pelayo), king of Asturia 61, 156
Pepin the Short 77, 161-2
Pericles 43, 149, 157
Persius 90, 167
Pertinax, Roman emperor 144, 199
Philalethes 24, 26

Philip of Macedon 60-1, 157, 167, 199
Phinehas 188
Pippin, see Pepin the Short
Plato 10, 62, 151, 152-4, 157, 158, 167, 168, 170, 171, 192
Pliny 153, 160
Plutarch 149, 154, 156, 158, 166, 170, 172, 179, 194
Ponet, John 9
Procopius 174
Prometheus 126
Pufendorf, Samuel 23

Quintilian 160, 161, 170

Robert Bruce, king of Scots 16, 106, 180
Ruddiman, Thomas 19
Rutherford, Samuel 22-23

Sallust 170, 189, 197
Samuel 110-111, 155, 182
Sejanus, Roman emperor 175
Sempronius 134, 196
Seneca 33, 62, 87, 148, 153, 157, 158, 166, 173, 200
Shields, Alexander 23
Sidney, Algernon 23-24, 25
Sidney, Sir Philip 21, 23
Solomon 181
Solon 194-5
Spurius Cassius, consul 98, 141, 172
Stewart, Dugald 25-26, 27
Stewart, James, of Goodtrees 22-23
Stichus 134, 196
Strabo 151

Suetonius 163, 168, 170, 173, 197
Suleiman the Magnificent 178
Sulla, L. Cornelius 99, 169, 173-4

Tacitus 150, 198
Terence 154, 158, 165, 171
Thebe, wife of Alexander of Pherae 97-8, 141, 172, 197
Theodosius, Roman emperor 134-5, 145, 156, 197, 199
Theopompus, king of Sparta 104-5, 179
Tiberius, Roman emperor 111, 183
Timoleon of Corinth 97, 172, 197
Timon of Athens 48, 151
Tiridates, king of Persia 142, 198

Titius 134, 196
Titus, Roman emperor 144, 198-9
Tribonian 100, 174
Turner, Sir James 22

Valentinian, Roman emperor 134-5, 197
Valerius Asiaticus 142
Valla, Lorenzo 174
Vespasian, Roman emperor 144, 198
Virgil 151, 158

William of Orange 24

Xenophon 62, 154, 156, 157, 170
Xerxes 156

About the Saltire Society

The Saltire Society was founded in 1936 at a time when many of the distinctive features of Scotland and its culture seemed in jeopardy. Over the years its members, who have included many of Scotland's most distinguished scholars and creative artists, have fought to preserve and present the nation's cultural heritage so that Scotland might once again be a creative force in European civilisation. As well as publishing books and producing recordings the Society makes a number of national awards for excellence in fields as diverse as housing design, civil engineering, historical publication and scientific research. There are Saltire Society branches in many towns and cities in Scotland and beyond, and each year members organise dozens of lectures, seminars and conferences on important aspects of Scottish culture.

The Society has no political affiliation and welcomes as members all who share its aims. Further information from The Administrator, The Saltire Society, Fountain Close, 22 High Street, Edinburgh, EH1 ITF Telephone 0131 556 1836.

Alternatively, you can make contact by email at saltire@saltiresociety.org.uk. and visit the Society web site at www.saltire-society.demon.co.uk

Saltire Publications

J. G. Lockhart: *Adam Blair*   0 85411 096 8
Paul H Scott: *The Union: Why and How*   0 85411 097 6
Carla Sassi: *Why Scottish Literature Matters*   0 85411 082 8
J. M. Barrie: *A Window in Thrums*   0 85411 084 4
Paul H Scott: *Scotland Resurgent*   0 85411 083 6
Paul H Scott (ed.): *Spirits of the Age: Scottish Self Portraits*   0 85411 087 9
Paul H Scott (ed.): *The Saltoun Papers*   0 85411 081 X
Wemyss, Alice: *Elcho of the '45*   0 85411 080 X
Paul H Scott and George Bruce (eds.): *A Scottish Postbag*   0 85411 078 X

Alexander Broadie: *Why Scottish Philosophy Matters*   0 85411 075 5
Ian Campbell: *Thomas Carlyle*   0 85411 052 6
Thomas Crawford: *Boswell, Burns and the French Revolution*   0 85411 046 1
William Ferguson: *Scotland's Relations with England*   0 85411 058 5
Johan Findlay: *All Manner of People*   0 85411 076 3
John Galt: *Annals of the Parish/The Ayrshire Legatees/The Provost*   0 85411 074 7
Robert Garioch: *Complete Poetical Works* ed. Fulton   0 90426 593 5
Robert Garioch: *Garioch Miscellany* ed. Fulton   0 86334 057 1
John S. Gibson: *Edinburgh in the '45*   0 85411 067 4
Ian Grimble: *The Trial of Patrick Sellar*   0 85411 053 4
Ian Grimble: *Chief of Mackay*   0 85411 051 8
Ian Grimble: *The World of Rob Donn*   0 85411 062 3
William Neill: *Tales frae the Odyssey o Homer*   0 85411 049 6
David Purves: *A Scots Grammar: Scots Grammar and Usage*   0 85411 079 8
Murray Ritchie: *Scotland Reclaimed*   0 85411 077 1
Paul H. Scott: *Andrew Fletcher and the Treaty of Union*   0 85411 057 7
Paul H. Scott: *Walter Scott and Scotland*   0 85411 056 9
Paul H. Scott: *Still in Bed with an Elephant*   0 85411 073 9
Paul H Scott: *The Boasted Advantages*   0 85411 072 0
Raymond Vettese: *A Keen New Air*   0 85411 063 1

Saltire publications are available from BookSource, 50 Cambuslang
Road, Cambuslang, Glasgow G32 8NB. Telephone: 0845 370 0063
e-mail: *customerservice@booksource.net*